The
FOOLISHNESS
of GOD

THE PLACE OF REASON IN THE THEOLOGY OF MARTIN LUTHER

Siegbert W. Becker

AN
CLASSIC

NORTHWESTERN PUBLISHING HOUSE
MILWAUKEE, WISCONSIN

Fourth printing, 2012
Third printing, 2009
Second printing, 2005
Second edition, 1999

Cover image by Titian, Planet Art.

Library of Congress Card 82-80945
Northwestern Publishing House
1250 N. 113th St., Milwaukee, WI 53226-3284

© 1982 by Northwestern Publishing House.
Published 1982
Printed in the United States of America
ISBN 978-0-8100-0155-8

Contents

Foreword

"The world in its wisdom did not know God." (I Corinthians I)

In passing his verdict on reason, Luther agrees with the Apostle Paul and opposes the wisdom of men like the Prophet Mohammed, Pope Paul III and John Calvin. On the same grounds, namely, that it is contrary to reason, Mohammed ridiculed the doctrine of the Trinity, Paul III condemned the doctrine of justification by faith alone, and John Calvin rejected the doctrine of the real presence of Christ in the Lord's Supper.

Whether in the robes of academia or in the garb of common sense, reason, "the devil's bride," is dressed to go into battle against the gospel of Christ. And since the time of Cain, the most appealing theologians, apologists, philosophers and scientists (in short, the world's best and wisest men) have rallied to her side, supported her cause and worshiped at her altar.

Yet that faculty of the human mind called reason is a great, yes, God's "greatest and most important," gift to man and "a most useful servant in theology." Reason as such has by no means been abolished from the Christian church. But before it can enter there, it must be converted from a judge into a penitent, from a master into a servant, from a professor into a pupil—or, more precisely, from a pagan into a Christian.

It is true that the Bible teaches many things which oppose the evidence otherwise available to reason through the senses. (How many of us have personally witnessed the revitalization of a man four days dead?) Still, the doctrines of the Bible do not "tear reason apart." Reason can apprehend the message, which the Bible conveys in the understandable form of ordinary human language. The fault, then, lies not with the message, but with fallen man, who rejects it precisely because he understands it. Therefore reason, if it is to become a servant of God, must yield to faith.

Unlike scores of other Reformation scholars and the empirical theologians of our own day, Dr. Becker wisely enters the labyrinth of Luther's reflections on reason with a ball of thread: he lets Luther trace his own way and speak for himself. Thus our author not only enters, but also returns to give us a true description and a trustworthy map—one which, for all its reticularity, is surprisingly simple to follow.

Dr. Becker, in brief, has succeeded, where many have failed, in describing the true place of reason in historic Lutheran theology. To the wise men of this age it still will be, and must remain, nothing but foolishness. But "the foolishness of God is wiser than men," and in this foolishness, that is, in this wisdom, our faith shall stand.

John A. Trapp
Editor

Preface

The original draft of this treatise on the antirationalism of Luther's theology was written in 1957 and submitted by the author as partial fulfillment of the requirements for a Th.D. degree at Northern Seminary in Chicago.

Almost twenty years later the author was asked to deliver a series of lectures on Luther's view of reason at the Pastors' Institute of Wisconsin Lutheran Seminary in Mequon, Wisconsin. In preparation for those lectures he resurrected the dissertation. The lectures were in large measure based on several chapters in that work.

Later one of the editors of the Northwestern Publishing House suggested that the lectures be submitted for publication. They are therefore herewith presented in expanded form to the church with the prayer that they will help God's people to resist the blandishments of reason in matters of faith.

A word of gratitude is due to the Aid Association for Lutherans, which provided a scholarship grant to cover the cost of preparing the manuscript for publication and to the author's daughter-in-law, Denise Kolander Becker, for typing it. The author also would like to thank Concordia Publishing House for granting permission to incorporate the contents of his article, "Luther's Apologetics," which appeared in the October, 1958 issue of the *Concordia Theological Monthly.*

Siegbert W. Becker

The foolishness of God is wiser than men.

—I Corinthians 1:25

CHAPTER I

INTRODUCTION

Reason is a big red murderess, the devil's bride,[1] a damned whore, a blind guide, the enemy of faith,[2] the greatest and most invincible enemy of God.[3] Reason is God's greatest and most important gift to man,[4] of inestimable beauty and excellence, a glorious light,[5] a most useful servant in theology, something divine.[6] In terms like these Martin Luther gave his estimate of human reason.

Roland Bainton, in his popular biography of Martin Luther, speaks of the reformer's "stupefying irrationalities."[7] He is referring, of course, to the many cases where Luther expressed the truths of the Christian faith in the form of paradox. Luther boldly underscored the apparent contradictions which characterize a theology which is faithful to the Bible.

Luther's paradoxical view of reason is there for every Lutheran child to see already in the Small Catechism. In his explanation of the First Article of the Creed Luther lists reason as one of the great gifts of the Creator for which men ought to be grateful. However, in the explanation of the Third Article he makes it plain that human reason is helpless and deserves no share of the credit for the conversion of man. He says there, "I believe that I can not, by my own reason or strength, believe in Jesus Christ, my Lord, nor come to him."

From all this it is clear that a fair logical presentation of Luther's views on the subject of reason will be complex and thought-provoking. Neo-orthodox theologians have consistently misunderstood what Luther had to say in this matter. It is easy to oversimplify and to caricature Luther's position over against reason. It is still easier to misunderstand his meaning, especially if the spotlight falls only on one side of

Luther's paradoxical views. There is no doubt that on many grounds Luther can be classified as an antirationalistic theologian. But to see clearly what his brand of antirationalism involves, we have to keep in mind the characteristics of the age in which he lived.

The son of Hans and Margaretha Luther was born into a rationalistic age. It was an age that had lost confidence in the power of the Word of God. In spite of everything that may be said to the contrary, the Late Middle Ages were not an age of faith, at least, not of faith in God's Word. George Bernard Shaw was correct when he said that there is "no Rationalism so rationalistic as Catholic Rationalism."[8] And Catholic rationalism finds its roots in the scholastic climate into which Martin Luther was born.

The scholastic age manifested an idolatrous trust in the powers of reason. The scholastic teachers, with few exceptions, held that fallen man had retained the light of reason in an undamaged state. "Reason intercedes for the best"[9] was a common axiom of scholasticism. Luther himself gave this description of the scholastic theologians:

> They contend that reason has retained its light undamaged (integrum), and if there is anything vicious in [human] nature it is the inferior part only that is corrupt and drawn away by lust and evil desire, but the higher part has an inextinguishable and pure light.[10]

Because of its favorable estimate of reason, scholastic theology had concocted a synthesis of reason and theology. Luther complained that the whole of theology had degenerated into philosophy and sophistic nonsense.[11] He was sure that this marriage ought never to have taken place, and he expressed great concern over any attempt to mix theology and philosophy.[12] He drew a sharp line of demarcation between the two disciplines. Philosophy, he said, deals with matters known by human reason, but theology with things apprehended by faith.[13]

Toward the end of 1519 the faculty at Louvain issued a condemnation of Luther's writings. The first charge they raised against him was that they found in his works "a notorious slandering of philosophy and of all the teachers of the last four centuries."[14] In reply Luther said that they had dealt more lovingly with Aristotle, a godless heathen and enemy of the truth, than with him, whom they ought to have recognized as a brother in the faith in need of their help.[15] He was sure also that if he had not attacked their philosophy, if he had not touched "this ulcer," they would very likely not have condemned his books.[16] His criticism implied that they cared little for theology and were concerned only with maintaining a philosophical position.

The scholastic theologians, under the influence of Thomas Aquinas, held that it was possible by a rational, philosophical method to lead men to the very threshold of the mysteries of the Christian faith. In fact, they believed that it was possible to establish so much of Christian theology by rational argument that the final step of accepting the revelation of God in Scripture became relatively easy.

Luther was convinced that such a process could only lead men away from the truth. In a sermon on the coming of the wise men he points out that they found Christ through the Scriptures and not with their reason. But, he says, the universities do not see this and teach instead that reason is good and useful and even necessary for the discovery and recognition of Christian truth.[17] It was bad enough when theologians considered the church fathers to be sources of truth—but now they have fallen into such abysmal ignorance "that they teach that the light of nature and heathen skill are also a good way to discover truth."[18] To punish the papists for exalting the comments of the fathers over the bare Scriptures, God finally let them fall into the arms of Aristotle.[19]

In Luther's opinion, Aristotle was the villain. He called the Greek philosopher that "damned, proud, rascally heathen," "the destroyer and waster of the church,"[20] "the heathen beast,"[21] and much more. And this was not a judgment that he formed late in his career as reformer. Long before Luther saw clearly what was wrong with the Roman Church, he recognized that Aristotle was one of the causes of her degeneration. Early in 1517, a good half a year before posting the *Ninety-Five Theses*, Luther said that if Aristotle had not been flesh, he would consider him to have been a devil.[22] J. K. F. Knaake, in an editorial preface to Luther's theses against scholastic theology, alludes to the fact that the reformer began a commentary (no longer extant) on the first of Aristotle's Physics sometime before 1517, and he says,

> *Er wollte dem Gaukler, der so lange die Kirche genarrt, die Maske abreisen und ihn aller Welt in seiner Schande zeichen.* (He wanted to tear the mask off this trickster, who had made a fool of the church for so long, and show him to the world in all his shame.)[23]

The scholastic teachers had gone so far as to say that no one could hope to become a theologian of the Christian church unless he first mastered Aristotle.[24] But in the 43rd and 44th of a set of theses prepared for the disputation against scholastic theology Luther wrote,

> It is an error to say that without Aristotle one does not become a theologian. . . . Indeed, one does not become a theologian unless he first frees himself from Aristotle.[25]

In his reply to the attack of Catherinus, Luther described the situation in the European universities by saying that the rector of all the universities is

> not Christ, not the Holy Spirit, not an angel
> of the Lord, but an angel from hell, that is a
> dead man, and one of the damned dead. . . .
> It is certain that the dead and damned
> Aristotle rather than Christ is today the
> teacher of all the universities.[26]

And so it had come to pass that the theologians of the Christian church were the disciples of a heathen and knew nothing of Christ.[27] Moreover, they were proud of it. Luther said, "At that time, the man who could quote Aristotle frequently and Christ, the apostles or the prophets never, was considered among the papists to be very learned."[28]

Luther believed that the churchman who had to share the blame with Aristotle for the sad state of affairs was Thomas Aquinas. It was Thomas who had begun the custom of interpreting the Scriptures by Aristotle.[29] And it was the authority of Thomas that had elevated Aristotle to the position he occupied in the church of the Middle Ages.[30]

In 1521 James Latomus, a member of the Louvain faculty, published an attack on Luther's theology. In it he accused Luther of ingratitude toward Thomas, Alexander, and others. Luther answered that they deserved this from him. He wrote, "Indeed, I have given this as my advice, that a young man should flee philosophy and scholastic theology as the death of his soul."[31] In this reply to Latomus, Luther expressed his doubt as to whether Thomas ought to be considered a Christian. He said that he would sooner believe that Bonaventure was in heaven than that Thomas was there, for "Thomas is the author of many heretical writings and responsible for the rule of Aristotle, the destroyer of godly doctrine."[32] Thomas, Luther said at another time, is worth as much as a louse, and in all his works there is not a single word that could possibly lead men to faith in Christ.[33] A stronger condemnation cannot be spoken by an evangelical theologian.

Luther had acquired this attitude toward Thomas and Aristotle from his teachers at Erfurt. The leading theologians of that university were disciples of the *via moderna*, the new way, which held that the Scriptures alone were to be the source and norm of theology.[34] In their turn, the Erfurt theologians had learned this especially from William of Occam,[35] whom Luther considered to be the chief and the most gifted of all the scholastic teachers.[36] When Luther returned from the Leipzig debate in 1519, he stopped at the monastery in Erfurt overnight. In the evening he went to see his old teacher Trutvetter. The Erfurt professor was "indisposed," and Luther returned to his lodging, where he wrote a letter to Trutvetter in which he said that it was from him that he had learned to exalt the Scriptures.[37]

Because of expressions like this, some have ventured to classify Luther with the "Moderns" or the "Occamists." There can be no doubt that Luther owes much to Occam.[38] Many of Luther's views on the sole authority of Scripture and the incompetence of reason in theology can be found in Occam.[39] But neither Occam nor the Erfurt theologians were willing to allow the principle of the sole authority of Scripture to become operative in the church. For all practical purposes, the church remained the supreme authority for both Occam and the Erfurt professors.[40] Moreover, Luther early disassociated himself from the "Moderns," whom he also classified as Aristotelians. In his sermons on the Ten Commandments, delivered in 1518, he said that Aristotle had been quadrupled into Thomists, Scotists, Albertists, and the Moderns.[41]

Luther's animosity against Aristotle did not have a philosophical, but a theological, base. He did not categorically reject everything Aristotle said, but he objected to the misuse of Aristotle by the scholastic theologians. He claimed that the scholastics did not understand even one line of Aristotle.[42] He even had to criticize Lyra's interpretation of the Greek philosopher,[43] though Lyra was his favorite Bible commentator.

In his Christmas sermon in 1515 Luther said,

> See how well Aristotle can serve theology with his philosophy, if he is understood and applied not as he wished but in a better way.[44]

Even toward the close of his life he still found much to praise in Aristotle.[45] What Luther could not tolerate was the opinion of the scholastics that there was complete agreement between the doctrine of Christ and Paul and that of Aristotle. Such a view, he held, could arise only out of a complete misunderstanding of both Aristotle and Christ.

When Luther attacked Aristotle and Thomas and scholastic theology in general he was giving voice, not to a criticism of reason as such, but to his settled conviction that reason is incapable of discovering and incompetent to judge religious truth. Reason has its place in the area of natural science, and it can render a service even in theology, but it has absolutely no business

> to investigate the origin of the whole world, where it came from and where it is going, whether it has a beginning or existed from eternity, whether there is a supreme being over the world, who rules all things.[46]

Scholasticism had ascribed such capacities to reason.

Unless this scholastic exaltation of reason is kept in mind when reading Luther, it is easy to misread his fulminations

against reason—as the neo-orthodox theologians of our time
have misread them. Luther never doubted, as they do, that it is
possible to set down the truths of revelation in propositional
form. And he never doubted the ability of human reason to
grasp the meaning. But it is just at this point that neo-orthodoxy
has maltreated Luther. Luther's intention in attacking reason
was to defend the sole authority of Scripture in all matters of
faith. Neo-orthodoxy, however, has made "faith" the judge of
Scripture, on the plea that human language is too limited to
become the vehicle for setting forth the majestic truth of
God's Word. You cannot find that kind of antirationalism
anywhere in Luther. His enemy was a scholasticism which had
lost faith in the power of the Word to stand alone against all
its enemies—a scholasticism which therefore turned to reason
as the guide of man and the defender of the revelation of
God. This, to Luther, was its fatal error.

Today, however, we face a completely different problem. Some
of the proponents of neo-orthodoxy have gone so far as to
assert that there is no natural knowledge of God and no revelation of any kind in nature. This is done in spite of Paul's
assertion that men do know and are therefore without excuse
in their idolatry. But even more serious in its practical consequences for Christian theology is the neo-orthodox axiom
that human language can not be a vehicle of divine revelation.
It has become common in neo-orthodox circles to assert in
apparent piety that the truth of God is so high and so holy
that it can never be captured in human formulations, not even
the formulations of Scripture. For this reason neo-orthodoxy
has been called a "revolt against reason."

It has also become common practice in neo-orthodox circles to
set up a false antithesis between Christ (as the Word of God)
and the Scriptures. Neo-orthodox theologians generally deplore
what they call a tendency to define faith not as simple trust in
the grace of God in Christ but as agreement with a collection
of individual, isolated statements drawn from the Bible.

At first glance such an assertion appears to harmonize with orthodox Lutheranism. Every Lutheran worthy of the name wants faith to be and to remain a simple trust in the grace of God in Christ. And, of course, it is also possible to quote numerous individual, isolated Bible passages which no Lutheran would be inclined to equate with the Christian faith. The list might include:

1. "There is no God." (Psalm 14:1—an assertion made by a "fool")

2. "In the neighboring village you will find an ass tied together with her colt." (Matthew 21:2)

3. "Nineveh was a great city." (Jonah 3:3)

4. "The staves used to carry the ark were drawn out and laid on the floor of the temple." (I Kings 8:8)

But it is also obvious that there are isolated, individual statements drawn from the Bible which cannot be rejected without at the same time renouncing the Christian faith. Yet, many neo-orthodox theologians, while asserting that they have trust in the grace of God in Christ, are perfectly willing to say that the body of Christ may not really have become alive again on the third day. They will say that the Scriptural reports of the resurrection are so confused and so contradictory that we cannot know what really happened. They will even criticize Paul because he seeks in I Corinthians 15 to establish the truth of the resurrection by "rational proof" with an appeal to eyewitnesses. Yet Paul in that same chapter makes it perfectly clear that Christian faith as trust in the grace of God in Christ cannot exist side by side with a denial of the bodily resurrection of Christ.

In its "revolt against reason" neo-orthodoxy falsely separates Christian faith from the written Word just as it separates

Christ from the written Word. And in doing so, it usually claims to be true to Reformation principles.

It is true that orthodox Lutheranism, with Luther and the confessions of the Lutheran Church, has always stressed that true faith in Christ is essentially trust in the Savior and not a mere acceptance of the historical reports about his life. But this is not the same as the neo-orthodox saying that true faith is trust in Christ as opposed to the acceptance of certain statements of the Bible. The latter is a false antithesis. True Lutheranism has never held that it is possible to *deny* all the statements of the Bible and still to have faith in Christ. It has, on the other hand, always held that faith in Christ is the same as agreement with the statements of the Bible, or, to paraphrase Luther, "trust in the words and promises of God." When Luther spoke of the words and promises of God he clearly had in mind the statements of the Bible.

In this connection we ought to remember what the Lutheran confessions say—namely, that where there is no promise there can be no faith.[47] Justifying faith is faith in the promises of God. And we can display these promises as a collection of individual, isolated statements drawn from the Bible. Whole-hearted agreement with these statements would be identical with a simple trust in the grace of God in Christ. To believe in Christ means to believe what the Bible says about him. In that sense, saving faith is nothing else but agreement with statements of the Bible.

Every Lutheran who endorses Luther's *Small Catechism* as a correct exposition of the gospel, by the same token confesses that whoever believes the *words*, "Given and shed for you for the remission of sins," has what those words say and express. Trust in the words and trust in Christ are really one and the same thing. The whole Lutheran doctrine of the means of grace rests on that simple premise.

Neo-orthodoxy's distinction between faith in Christ and faith in statements, or "faith in a book," is artificial and contrary to reason. By rejecting "propositional revelation" and making the Bible only a "record of" and "witness to" revelation, the neo-orthodox theologians drain faith of its intellectual content. They make it little more than an emotional response to a "divine self-disclosure" which takes place not through the words of Scripture, though possibly in conjunction with them.

Emil Brunner, for example, says that

> faith means to be gripped by the Word of God [by this he does not mean the words of Scripture]; it means that a person submits in the very center of his being, in his heart, to Him to whom he belongs, because He has created him for Himself. . . . But this does *not* mean an intellectual understanding, *but* a personal encounter. [emphasis added][48]

The false antithesis which Brunner sets up here is one against which we must always be on our guard. In positing such a sharp distinction between "intellectual understanding" and "personal encounter" (some call it "total commitment"), neo-orthodoxy betrays its Calvinistic and Zwinglian roots.

The *Formula of Concord* teaches that the assurance of our faith is to be based on the fact that God's grace and the promise of the gospel are universal and that this promise is made in all earnestness by God.[49] Since Calvinism rejects the universality of the gospel promise, a consistent Calvinist can never find assurance in that promise. Instead, he seeks it within the experience of his conversion, or, in neo-orthodox terms, in his "personal encounter" with God, who speaks directly to the heart.

Luther, on the other hand, always exalted the Word. The Holy Spirit, according to Luther, does not wish to deal with us other than through the spoken Word and the sacraments.[50] The faculties of human reason are therefore necessary to grasp and to understand what the Word proclaims. It is true that Luther displayed a deep distrust in human reason and saw reason as the greatest enemy of faith. Yet he never disparaged intellectual understanding of the gospel—which is also a function of reason. While Luther always acknowledged faith to be the confidence of the heart, he also said that "faith is in the intellect."[51]

While the great Reformer may be correctly classified as an antirationalist in one sense, this antirationalism is not at all related to the neo-orthodox revolt against reason and its brand of antirationalism. It will be our aim in the following chapters to demonstrate this from Luther's own writings and in his own words.

CHAPTER II

NATURAL THEOLOGY IN LUTHER

As a result of the Kantian revolution in philosophy and the Barthian upheaval in theology it has become fashionable in the theological world of our time to attack the whole concept of natural theology. Those who have taken this position have often tried to claim Luther and the other reformers as sharers of their point of view. And they have been so successful in propagating their cause that a modern writer feels constrained to apologize for even suggesting that "anything like natural theology might be found in Luther."[1]

THE HIDDEN GOD

It is impossible to understand Luther's views on natural theology clearly without a firm prior grasp of his entire concept of God *(Gottesbegriff)* and of the nature of man.[2]

Luther held that there is no way in which man can find God in his divine majesty. He said that it is possible that God appeared in his bare majesty to Adam before the Fall. But since the Fall man has, and can have, no direct knowledge of God. Since the Fall, God is a hidden God.[3] God is everywhere, Luther said, but is certainly not to be found in our speculations about him nor in the pictures that we form of him in our thoughts and senses. God is everywhere, but he permits men to grasp him nowhere.[4]

When Luther speaks of this hidden God,[5] he emphasizes especially God's absolute control over all creation. Here he speaks as emphatically and as eloquently as Calvin about the sovereignty and the majesty of God. But he holds that we can know nothing of this God. When we deal with this hidden

God and his mysterious will, we are not to be curious; our sole duty is to adore with reverential awe. Here we are confronted by mysteries which God has reserved for himself and hidden from us. In his answer to the *Diatribe* of Erasmus,[6] Luther writes:

> We must speak in one way about God and the will of God which is preached, revealed, shown openly, and worshiped and in another way about the God who is not preached, not revealed, not shown openly, and not worshiped. Insofar therefore as God hides himself from us and wishes to be unknown by us, he is nothing to us. . . . The *Diatribe* makes itself ridiculous by its ignorance in making no distinction between God as preached and God as hidden, that is, between the Word of God and God himself. God does many things which he does not make known to us in his Word. He also wills many things which he does not in his Word reveal himself as willing. Thus God does not will the death of the sinner so far as his Word is concerned, but he does will this in his unsearchable will. Now, however, we must keep our eyes on the Word and not on that unsearchable will. By the Word we must be directed, not by that inscrutable will.[7]

Luther anticipated that others would criticize his sharp distinction between "the revealed God" and "the hidden God" as a mere subterfuge and a clever attempt to avoid a clear and definite solution to some of the difficult problems with which we are confronted in our thinking about God. He said that reason compares this concept of a hidden God to the epicycles which the Ptolemaic astronomers posited to resolve all their difficulties in explaining the movements of the heavenly bodies. He had no answer to this criticism except to say that he was only repeating what the Scriptures say in Romans 9 and Isaiah 58.[8]

Because God is a God who hides himself, we are not to seek him out by our speculations. To seek him in this way is fraught with danger. "Nothing is more dangerous," Luther says, "than to build one's own road to God and to climb up by our own speculations."[9] What he calls the *sensum speculativum*[10] must be held in check.[11] Those who seek God in this way will always fall into error; their reason will always seek in vain.[12] The questions which arise from that curiosity which pries into the inscrutable wisdom of God are full of danger and destruction. Adam sought God this way in the garden, and the devil did the same in heaven, and "they both found him, but not without great damage."[13] For this reason speculative theology belongs to the devil in hell.[14]

Not only is such speculation dangerous, but it is also very foolish. Men can gain nothing by it. When once we seek an answer to our questions about God in this way, "the questions will multiply in direct proportion to the time spent on them, and there will be more questions than sand on the sea shore."[15] Therefore, according to Luther,

> What God does not want revealed, that I am not to know. . . . If I am not to know it, I should be quiet—or else I will break my neck. What God has not revealed you can not understand, even if you tear yourself to pieces over it. Therefore be on your guard against this very common temptation of wanting to know. "Why does God do this?" Friend, watch out for that "Why?" or you will break your neck. . . . On this apple we all still choke.[16]

This warning against all speculation in regard to the deity is one which is often repeated in Luther's writings. In 1532, when he was very sick and felt that the end was near, he said,

> If I can leave behind me what I have taught with all diligence, namely, that one should beware of speculation and only hold to Christ in all simplicity, I shall have accomplished much.[17]

At first it may appear that Luther is here denying all natural knowledge of God. But, in fact, these remarks of Luther regarding a "hidden God" tell us absolutely nothing about his views on the natural knowledge of God. The contrast for Luther is not one between natural knowledge and revealed knowledge. The hidden God is not the God who is unknown until he reveals himself. He remains hidden even when he reveals himself. At first glance, this may look like a typical Barthian paradox. When Luther spoke of the hidden God he had in mind the God who proclaims his name to Moses and yet says, "No man shall see my face and live." The term "hidden God" refers to those aspects of God's essence and operation which he simply has chosen not to reveal to us. Some things about God are revealed and some are never revealed. The question therefore that needs to be answered is this: When we speak of God as revealed must we limit that revelation to the written and spoken Word, or is there also a revelation of God in nature? This question becomes easier to answer if we consider what Luther has to say about the "masks of God."

THE MASKS OF GOD

According to Luther God does not hide himself because he wants to remain undiscovered and unknown to us. In a sermon which he preached in Wittenberg early in 1517 he said, "A man hides what he is in order to deny it; God hides what he is in order to reveal it."[18] God knows that fallen man can never know him in his bare majesty, for he dwells in the light that no man can approach.[19] God in his mercy hides from us that which would destroy us if we were to gaze at it. Nevertheless God wants us to know him. This, Luther says, is clear from his command that his Word should be preached in all the world to all creatures.[20]

Even though man cannot know God in his majesty, yet it is God's earnest desire that all men should know him. For this reason God disguises himself and puts on a mask, as it were. This makes it possible for man to look at him and live. After man fell into sin God no longer appeared in his bare majesty to Adam, but made his presence known in the sound of the breeze blowing through the garden. The breeze thus becomes one of the "masks" of God.[21] This way of speaking, if it is pressed for all it is worth, would seem to be of tremendous significance in evaluating Luther's concept of natural theology. Through the rustling of the leaves God is able to make Adam conscious of his condemning presence, just as the heavens declare the glory of God. Apparently Luther believed that God revealed himself in more ways in nature than even many modern proponents of natural theology would care to admit.

This employment of "masks" by God in his act of revelation is found also in the area of what we usually call "special revelation." Luther writes,

> Afterwards, in the tabernacle God revealed himself at the mercy seat, and in the desert he showed himself in the cloud and in the fire. For that reason Moses called these things the "face" of God, through which God manifested himself, and Cain called the place where he had formerly sacrificed "the face of God." For this nature of ours is so deformed, so corrupt and ruined by sin that

> it is not able to grasp what sort of God he is
> in his bare majesty. Therefore these disguises
> are necessary.[22]

It is evident that Luther holds that God to a certain degree hides himself behind these "masks" and "disguises" himself in this way in order that he might reveal himself to us, who can neither tolerate nor grasp the direct revelation of his unbounded majesty.

For the same reason the Scriptures also speak of God in human terms. Such anthropomorphisms, in which God is spoken of as though he had the form of a man, are, according to Luther, part and parcel of God's mode of revealing himself to us in a way which we can grasp.[23] Most interesting is Luther's remark that such anthropomorphisms are foreshadowings of the incarnation in which God actually takes on the form of a man, that we might have "a sure way *(certam formam)* of knowing and laying hold of God."[24] To these disguises in which God makes himself known to us belong also the covenant of circumcision in the Old Testament and the word and sacraments in the New Testament.[25]

It is the height of folly to search out the bare majesty of the hidden God apart from these masks in which God comes to men. Those who want to come into contact with God without these masks *(involucra)* are trying to climb into heaven without a ladder, that is, without the Word.[26]

When the Bible speaks of God, Luther says, it describes him as a voice, as a dove, as revealing himself to us in the water of baptism and in the bread and wine of the Lord's Supper. Everyone knows that God is not a voice, not a dove, not water, not bread, not wine. And yet God offers himself to us in those forms. We can not lay hold of him in his bare majesty, but under these forms we can grasp him. They are our Urim and

Thummim.[27] Only those who are satisfied with these apparently simple and seemingly unworthy appearances and manifestations of God will truly find him. But those who insist on visions and new revelations either will be crushed by the divine majesty or will wander about in the deepest ignorance of God even though they imagine that they have found him. From the bare majesty of God we must shield our eyes, for we cannot apprehend it. It is God's will to appear to us only in the masks, that is, in baptism, the Word, and the sacrament of the altar. These are the divine portraits (*simulachra*) through which he deals with us for our understanding. These masks are the way in which we must seek all our knowledge of the Lord.[28] Therefore, Luther concludes,

> it is madness to dispute about God and the divine nature without the Word and a disguise of some kind, as all heretics are accustomed to doing. They speculate about God with the same freedom from anxiety with which they dispute about a pig or a cow.[29]

The supreme disguise in which God reveals himself to men is the incarnation. We have already noted that Luther sees the anthropomorphisms of Scripture as a foreshadowing of the incarnation of God.[30] In the *Table Talk* he is quoted as saying,

> No one can grasp or know God in his majesty. Therefore he came down in lowly form, became a man, yes, was made to be sin, and death, and weakness itself. He became small, when he took on the form of a servant, as St. Paul says to the Philippians. But who can believe it? We imagine that the Turkish sultan is much more powerful, Erasmus much more learned, and a monk much more pious than God.[31]

We will find God when we seek him in the arms of the Virgin and in the manger of Bethlehem.[32] If men want to know what the will of God is concerning them, let them listen to Mary's Son. Outside of him God has locked up his heart and has hidden his will.[33]

However, the masks of God include not only the incarnation, the means of grace, and the methods of revelation that God employed in the Bible and Biblical history. Luther saw the natural world also as one of the masks of God. Just as God hides himself in the means of grace, so he hides his invisible attributes in the whole world of nature. All the works of God are such masks behind which we see God at once hidden and revealed.[34] If men could see correctly and clearly, they would see God in all of his creatures.[35] In his Genesis lectures, Luther said,

> God does not manifest himself except in his
> works and in his Word, because these, in a
> way, can be grasped. The other things which
> belong to his divinity cannot be grasped and
> understood as they really are. . . . For that rea-
> son God wraps himself in his works and cer-
> tain types of things, as today he has wrapped
> himself in baptism, in absolution, etc.[36]

While we find the clearest revelation of God in the incarna-tion of Jesus Christ and in Word and sacrament, yet every work of God, every creature, reveals something of God. "The footsteps of God are in the creature."[37] Created things, too, are therefore masks behind which God hides himself so that we may see him.

It should be noted that Luther never implies that there is anything inadequate about these masks of God. They are the only instruments that are indeed adequate to suit the situation when the Creator seeks to communicate with men. They represent the only way in which God can make himself known to sinful men without destroying them by the glory of his majesty. If there is any inadequacy in the whole process, Luther ascribes it to men, who look at all the works of God as a cow stares at a new gate.[38]

THE INCOMPETENCE OF MAN

Our miserable state is a result of the Fall, which blighted man's power of understanding and reason. Reason itself was not lost in the Fall, but it became corrupt. Even after the Fall, Luther observes, reason remains the most beautiful and excellent gift of all, but it lies captive in the power of the devil. What has been lost in the Fall is not reason but the image of God.[39] In disagreement with the church fathers and also with many of the subsequent dogmaticians of the Lutheran Church, both early and late, Luther vigorously insists that these two concepts, reason and the image of God, are not at all related. He categorically rejects the teaching of Augustine, who held that the image of God consists of the powers of the soul, the memory, the intellect, and the will. This view, which generally held by the theologians of the Middle Ages, Luther calls "a dangerous opinion." He says that even though we have lost the image of God we still have the gifts of memory,[40] intellect, and will, and that if these powers were the image of God, then it would follow that the devil, who has these powers in a far higher degree than we, also has retained the image of God.[41] The devils are more clever, more rational, and wiser than all men, yet they are not better on that account.[42] What has happened through the Fall is this that the memory, the intellect, and the will of man have become very corrupt, yes, completely leprous and unclean. Luther continues,

> Therefore the image of God is a far different thing—indeed, an extraordinary work of God. The image of God, in which Adam was created, was a very outstanding and noble thing, a state in which no leprosy of sin

inhered either in the reason or in the will, but
both the interior and the exterior senses were
all the very finest. The intellect was most
pure, the memory the best, the will most
upright, in the most beautiful freedom from
anxiety, without any fear of death and completely without worry. . . . Therefore when we
speak of the image of God, we speak of an
unknown thing. We have no experience of it.
But we always experience the very opposite.
We hear nothing of it but empty vocables.
For there was in Adam an enlightened reason,
a true knowledge of God, and an upright will
which loved God and the neighbor.[43]

In a similar way Luther also rejected the ancient idea of the
Logos which the philosophically inclined church fathers had
again introduced. They maintained that a universal reason
resides in every man. Luther called this a human, Platonic,
philosophical conception which leads us away from the Lord
Jesus Christ. What the ancients said about such an indwelling
universal reason was useless and silly chatter; by it they led
Augustine and, through Augustine, the whole church astray.[44]

Because reason is totally corrupt, it sees nothing correctly.
Because the intellect is completely depraved, it fails to understand the revelation of God. Because the will is entirely evil, it
does not want to find God behind the masks. Here, in the total
depravity of the whole human nature, we find the real reason
why men do not know God. Against the Semi-pelagianism of
the scholastic theologians Luther held that all the spiritual
powers of man were entirely destroyed by sin. So that nothing
remains in man but

a depraved intellect and will, inimical and
opposed to God, which is able to think
nothing except what is contrary to God.

> Whatever is in our will is evil. Whatever is in
> our intellect is error.[45]

If natural reason were right, he says, we would judge rightly.[46] It is very evident that the revelation of God is there behind the masks for all men to see. The same evidence is presented to all men. They all see the same works of God. They all hear the same Word of God. But the trouble lies completely in our depravity. If Adam and Eve had not fallen into sin, both they and their descendants would have retained a knowledge of efficient and final causes, but now men know as little of them as cattle do.[47] When Luther says that men would know efficient causes, he means above all else that men would have a true and correct knowledge of the Creator.

Since the Fall our reason sees all things through red or blue glasses, and everything it sees must either be red, or blue, or green.[48] What Luther means when he speaks in this way is that our whole attitude with which we discuss divine things is wrong. Men want to talk about such matters when they are sitting in their club or in a tavern, while they are waiting for their wine or beer.[49] They simply refuse to take God's revelation seriously. Such is the perversity of the human heart that men with far greater ease and eagerness embrace other gods rather than this God who reveals himself in promises and signs.

> And what is the cause? It is this wickedness
> inborn in us through original sin by which
> our soul always rebels against the promises of
> God, murmurs and says, "God lies; his oath
> is not true."[50]

In his commentary on Genesis Luther describes the fallen state of man in these words:

> Man has fallen from the image of God, from
> the knowledge of God, from the knowledge

of all other creatures, from an honest naked-
ness into blasphemies, into hatred, into con-
tempt of God, yes, what is more, into enmity
against God. . . . How can one speak of a
right reason that hates God? How can one
speak of a good will which resists the will of
God and refuses to obey God? . . . However,
it is common knowledge that when the
knowledge of God is preached (and this is
done that reason may be restored), then the
best men, and those who have the better reason and will, if I may speak in this way, hate
the gospel so much more bitterly. And so in
theology we should say that reason in man is
filled with hatred of God.[51]

If men at their very best are enemies of God, if the sharpest
intellects reject the wisdom of God, then what shall we expect
from those who are less intelligent and less pious? In a sermon
on the visit of Nicodemus to Jesus, Luther says,

If Nicodemus, who was a pious and good
man, cannot understand God's work and
Word, how shall Annas and Caiaphas understand it?[52]

If we are to understand what Luther has to say in the area of
natural theology, we have to bear in mind his views concerning
the total intellectual corruption of man.

THE PROOFS FOR GOD'S EXISTENCE

On the basis of statements such as the foregoing, which are
rather common in Luther's writings, some have concluded that
the whole concept of natural theology is completely foreign to
him. This opinion, however, is completely unjustified. Rudolph
Thiel cannot be accused of misquoting Luther when he writes,
"In mature years he testified that reason must conclude on

philosophical grounds that 'there is no God at all.'"[53] Yet, that sentence gives an inexcusably wrong impression.

It is true that the great Reformer completely denied both the premises and the conclusions of Thomas Aquinas. As we have seen, Luther looked upon Thomism as nothing more than pagan Aristotelianism with a Christian veneer. In fact, he considered Thomas to be far worse than Aristotle, for Aristotle at least did not pretend to be a Christian as Thomas did.

Watson, in his book, *Let God Be God!*,[54] which is in many ways an excellent treatment of one aspect of Luther's theology, says,

> Luther, it is certain, has little if any place for the conception which finds classical expression in Aquinas and has been traditionally maintained by both the Roman and Protestant theologians, that a certain definite knowledge of God can be attained by rational inference from the world of nature. This type of natural theology deriving ultimately from the theistic argumentation of Plato and Aristotle, treats the existence and, in large measure, the nature and attributes of God as conclusions to be established by means of argument. The "natural" knowledge thus gained by the exercise of "reason" is not claimed, it is true, as a complete knowledge of God; but what is lacking in it can be made up by supernatural "revelation."[55]

While there is much that is perfectly true in this point of view, yet there is one essential feature in Luther's treatment of the "proofs" for God's existence which we should not ignore. Everywhere Luther recognizes that the "proofs" have a great deal of validity and force. Luther believed that God has revealed himself in his works. He believed that God has left a record in nature for all men to read. "The footsteps of the Godhead are in the creature," he says. Luther never sharply distinguished between what we call "natural revelation" and what we call "the natural proofs for the existence of God." The modern distinction made between them seems to be foreign to Luther's thought. It just never occurred to him.

But, be that as it may, it remains impossible to understand Luther's view in this matter except against the background of his doctrine of human depravity. Contrary to the approach of neo-orthodoxy, Luther held that the fault for man's failure to know God and to read the record correctly lies not at the doorstep of the revelation, whether in the works or in the Word, but in the depravity of human nature.

It would be difficult, for example, to imagine Luther agreeing with the views of John Hutchison, who writes,

> Concerning their subjective or persuasive force, it may be pointed out that the arguments, while they tend to sustain the faith of those already convinced of belief in God, are seldom convincing to those without that faith. It is characteristic of genuine proof that it communicates conviction to minds hitherto unconvinced. What kind of proofs are they which lack this quality? It is difficult to avoid the conclusion that they are covertly circular, assuming what they ought to conclude.[56]

There are many things here that Luther would have criticized sharply. For one thing, he would never have admitted that you have told the whole story when you say, as Hutchison does, that the proofs "tend to sustain the faith of those already convinced." Luther knew all too well that man here is involved in a conflict of interest. The evidence that may convince the

whole world that John Jones is a bank robber may not be sufficient to convince John Jones' mother of the same fact. The
evidence which may have "already convinced" almost the
whole world of the existence of God may not be sufficient to
convince the man who has a personal stake in the non-existence
of an almighty Judge of his every word and deed.

But most of all, Luther would have found fault with the
basic wrong-headedness of this view. He would never have
asked, as Hutchison does, "What kind of proofs are these
which lack this quality?" He just did not think that way.
Instead Luther would have asked, "How fallen, how blind,
and how wicked is man, that he can not and he will not see
what God has so clearly and so graciously revealed!" In the
final analysis, Luther and Hutchison and neo-orthodox
theologians agree that natural man is without sure and
certain knowledge of God, but they would undoubtedly
disagree vehemently on the premise on which that conclusion
is built. Neo-orthodoxy would say that man lacks faith in
God because no revelation has taken place. Luther would say
that man lacks sure knowledge because he refuses the revelation. In spite of everything that has been written since
Kierkegaard became the fashion in theology, the "proofs,"
for Luther, have a great deal more validity than is commonly
supposed. This is not difficult to establish.

LUTHER'S PLATONISM

Very early in his career as reformer, at the Heidelberg
Disputation in May of 1518, Luther already gave a clear indication of the direction which his thought in these matters
would take. The thirty-sixth of the theses drawn up by Luther
for this disputation says, "Aristotle acts wickedly when he
rejects and ridicules the Platonic ideas, a better philosophy
than his own." [57]

It would not be fair to Luther, however, to call his position in
the matter of natural theology a Platonic rationalism, and

Luther would have been the first to reject any such suggestion.
He recognized that there were some things on which he could
agree with Plato, but he believed, as many of the church
fathers believed before him, that Plato had stolen whatever was
wise and good in his writings from those who had a true
knowledge of God. In the introductory remarks to his
commentary on Genesis he says that Plato very likely gleaned
a few sparks of light out of the sermons of the prophets and
the fathers, and for that reason he came closer to the truth
than Aristotle.[58]

In one of his sermons Luther observed,

> If the natural law were not written in the
> heart and given by God, one would have to
> preach a long time before the conscience
> would be touched. . . . But because it is previ-
> ously written in the heart, although it is dark
> and completely faded, it is reawakened by the
> Word, so that the heart must confess that
> what the commandment says is right: that
> one should honor a God, love and serve him,
> because he alone is good and does good not
> only to the pious but also to the wicked.[59]

It is evident that Luther would sooner have agreed with the
Platonic doctrine of anamnesis than with the dictum of
Aquinas, "There is nothing in the intellect which is not previ-
ously in the senses."

In 1526 Luther published a commentary on Jonah. In
commenting on the prayers of the sailors during the storm, he
said that this action shows that God is known to the heathen.
They know that God is a Being who can help in time of need:

> Such light and understanding is in the heart
> of all men and is not easily smothered or

extinguished. There have indeed been some, such as the Epicureans, Pliny, and the like, who deny it with the mouth. But they do it with force and want to smother the light in their hearts. They act as those who forcibly plug up their ears and hold their eyes shut so that they neither see nor hear. But it does no good; their conscience tells them otherwise. For Paul does not lie when he says that God has revealed it to them, so that they know something about God. For these people believe that God is a Being who can help in all time of need. Out of that it follows that natural reason must confess that all good comes from God. . . . The natural light of reason goes this far: it considers God to be good, gracious, merciful, and kind. That is a great light.[60]

In the same connection Luther says that there is a great difference between knowing that there is a God and knowing who or what God is. "The first is known by nature and is written in all hearts," he says. "But the other is taught only by the Holy Ghost."[61]

Eleven years after the publication of the commentary on Jonah, in which he expressed himself so clearly and definitely on the subject of natural theology, Luther preached a sermon on John 1:18 which manifests the same point of view. In that sermon he said that all the heathen know that murder, adultery, theft, lying, cursing, cheating and blaspheming are wrong. They are conscious also of the existence of a God who punishes such wickedness.[62] In the same sermon he goes on to say that to know that there is a God is natural knowledge common to all men. Such knowledge, he says, grows out of reason, for it is written in us.[63]

THE ONTOLOGICAL "PROOF"

The innate knowledge of God, however, even when it is firm and stable, is greatly limited. In the area of what we would call natural theology Luther distinguished between an *a priori* knowledge of God and an *a posteriori* knowledge. The first is inborn. The second is a conclusion of reason. We know very little *a priori*. The *a posteriori* knowledge is far more extensive,[64] as we shall see, but much less stable.

Luther treats the knowledge of God as a universal historical phenomenon. All men know that there is a God. This is a truism about which he never had any doubt. But he is not too much interested in this knowledge as a question in philosophy. He considered the scholastic disputations about the question a waste of time.[65] He says in one place that in the universities there has been a great deal of needless concern over the question whether a man is able by his natural powers to know God.[66] To Luther the question was not one to be decided by philosophical debate. The natural knowledge of God is simply a fact—an item of divine revelation. And the testimony of history simply bears out Paul's statement in Romans I. In the 1535 edition of his Galatians commentary Luther wrote,

> All men naturally have this general knowl-
> edge that there is a God according to
> Romans I. . . . Then also the worship and
> the religions, which have been and still are
> found among all the heathen, testify suffi-
> ciently to this that all men have a certain
> general knowledge of God, whether truly by
> nature or by tradition from their parents,
> I am not now disputing.[67]

The last remark is interesting, but isolated. I am unaware of any other passage where Luther raises the same question. The evidence we do have indicates that Luther favored the view that this general knowledge came by nature, not primarily by tradition.

The existence of God, so far as Luther is concerned, is simply a fact known to all men without exception. In the *Large Catechism* we have his well-known remark that no people has ever been so reckless that it did not establish and observe some form of divine worship. In his commentary on Jonah he wrote,

> Here you see that what St. Paul says in Romans I is true, that God is known among all the heathen. All the world knows how to speak of the deity, and natural reason recognizes that the Godhead is something great and above all other things.[68]

In another place he wrote,

> What St. Paul says to the Romans is true, that God has revealed to the whole world that they must know that there is a God. . . . There must be a God—this they knew, and they were right.[69]

Notice here that Luther says the heathen *must* know that there is a God. Someone might say that this is Luther's form of the ontological proof, although someone else could with justification argue that it should not be called a "proof," or even an "argument." For, in the opinion of Luther, the knowledge of God is a truism, a plain and evident fact which confronts us when we study the history of the world. No one really needs to have it "proved" to him. It needs only to be stimulated into consciousness.

THE COSMOLOGICAL AND TELEOLOGICAL "PROOFS"

But this is still not to say that Luther saw no validity in the "proofs" for the existence of God. It is still true that to Luther the cosmological argument was more than an "analogical essay," as J. V. Langmead Casserley calls it.[70] And it is possible to question the complete correctness of the assertion of Philip Watson that

> Romans 1:20 . . . is not, as Aquinas thought, an example of the argument from design; for what is said is not that God's existence can be proved from His works, but that in and through them certain aspects of His nature—"His eternal power and divinity"— are revealed. That is precisely Luther's teaching; and with it he anticipates some of the best modern thought on the subject.[71]

But does this "precisely" represent where Luther stands? Luther, for example, sees human government as an analogy by which we can come to some conception of God's nature and attributes. Just as we look at a castle or a house from the outside and thus have some conception of the lord or the private citizen who dwells within, so we may look at the world and gain some conception of God.[72] The ancient Greek poet Homer, Luther adds, made mention of the fact that there can be no good government where there is more than one governor, and Aristotle concluded from this that there must be one God who governs the world. Luther says that this is a conclusion reached on "reasonable grounds" (vernunfftigen ursachen).[73] He writes,

> This is surely right and true, for God has planted such light and understanding in human nature that it may be an indication and, as it were, a picture of his divine government, that he is a single Lord and Creator of all creatures.[74]

Luther treats the cosmological and teleological proofs, which he never seems to differentiate from one another, with much more respect than Watson would seem to indicate. Luther categorically states (and this is from one of the last sermons he preached), "That there is a God, by whom all things were made, you know from his works, that is, from yourself and all creatures."[75] Human reason, he says, can conclude and recognize from God's works that God must be one eternal essence, Creator of all things, wise and just.[76] While human nature is blinded by sin, it can still "smell" God in his works.[77] By the use of reason the heathen can know that the certain orderly course of the heavenly bodies could not have its stability or its being without a ruler; and we can recognize the invisible nature of God, his eternal power and Godhead, if we pay attention to his works.[78]

From all this it is evident that Luther considered the cosmological argument to be of some significance. His apparent lack of concern about these arguments is not due to a lack of confidence in their validity. He looks upon them as having compelling force. We have already noted his use of the word "must" in this connection. In a comment on Psalm 129, on which he lectured in 1533, he said, "We are *forced* to ascribe to God omnipotence, wisdom, and goodness."[79] And in 1537 he wrote,

> Human reason and wisdom by itself can come this far, that it concludes, although weakly, that there must be a single, eternal divine Being, which has created, preserves, and governs all things. When reason considers such beautiful, exquisite creatures both in heaven and earth, governed in such a wonderful, orderly and sure way, it must deny the possibility that the origin and preservation of these things are accidental or spontaneous. There must be a Creator and Lord from whom all things came and by whom all are governed. And so reason must know God by his creatures, as St. Paul says in Romans I.[80]

It is very evident from these words that Luther did not reject, nor did he despise, the "proofs." In his commentary on Genesis he discusses the treatment of the cosmological and teleological arguments in Cicero and Aristotle in these words,

> Although I hold that Aristotle was more gifted than Cicero, yet I see that Cicero has argued much more wisely about these things. . . . For he leads the argument to a consideration of the created world, which in a way is subject to the judgment of reason. For he sees the harmonious motions of the heavenly bodies, the regular succession of the seasons, the well developed forms of the species, and he sees that man was created for this that he should understand and enjoy these things. From this he comes to the conclusion that God is eternal Mind, by whose providence all things are governed, and that the soul of man is immortal.[81]

Earlier in the same commentary he had written,

> You see that in some places the philosophers do not debate in an unskillful way about God and providence, by which God governs all things. To some their words seem to be so pious that they very nearly make prophets out of Socrates, Xenophon, and Plato.[82]

THE MORAL "PROOF"

In addition to the ontological, cosmological, and teleological "proofs," Luther takes note also of the moral "proof" for the existence of God. The so-called "moral proof" is always difficult to differentiate from the idea of an inborn, *a priori* knowledge of God. We have already taken note of several remarks of the reformer in which he alludes to the fact that men know that there is a God who punishes sin, and in which he speaks of the testimony of the conscience to God's existence even in those who deny his existence with the mouth.[83] In his sermon on John 1:18 he treats this matter in some detail in the following words:[84]

> The knowledge of the law is known to reason, and reason has almost touched and smelled God. For they saw out of the law what was right and wrong, and the law is written in our hearts, as St. Paul testifies to the Romans. Although it is more clearly revealed through Moses, it is nevertheless also true that by nature all rational men can come this far that they know that to disobey father and mother or the government is wrong—likewise murder, adultery, theft, cursing, and blasphemy. . . . So far reason can go in knowing God that it has a law knowledge. It knows God's command and what is right and wrong. The philosophers also had this knowledge of God.[85]

He goes on to say that the knowledge of the heathen is better than that of the monks with their moral juggling. The heathen came closer than the monks to finding God, because they at least retained the commands of God and knew what God required of them, while the monks invented their own works. Luther concludes, "The heathen and all the wise men and the philosophers have come so far as to know God through the law."[86]

GEORGE MAJOR'S THESES

As a final exhibit to show that Luther did not reject the "proofs," we may take note of a disputation that was held at the University of Wittenberg in December of 1544 on the occasion of the promotion of George Major and John Faber to the doctorate. Luther served as presiding officer at the debate.[87] Major submitted a series of theses for the disputation. In them he dealt with the way in which God is known. Since Major was closely associated with the University of Wittenberg from 1511, when he was only nine years old, we may assume that the viewpoint of Luther is at least to some extent mirrored in these theses.

As we would expect, Major begins with Scripture and the doctrine of creation, a course which is certainly in harmony with the approach Luther takes to the question. We have seen how often Luther refers to Romans 1 in this connection. But after the Scripture-oriented beginning, Major continues as follows:

> There are also other indications of God.
>
> 1) The certain order of things.
>
> 2) Human reason is . . . suitable for discussing the divine nature (*par divinae naturae*). Therefore God is the author of reason in man.
>
> 3) The ability to distinguish between good and evil man does not have from himself or by chance. Therefore there must be a God from whom it is derived.
>
> 4) Natural knowledge.
>
> 5) Man's horror of great crimes testifies to the existence of a God who punishes crimes.
>
> 6) The conservation of human society.
>
> 7) Prophecies are not from men, but from God. Therefore there is a God.

LUTHER AND PROBABILITY

While it is clear therefore that Luther did not deny that there was such a thing as natural theology and an objective revelation of God in nature, and while he did not consider the so-called "proofs" unworthy of notice, yet he laid little stress on this natural knowledge for several reasons.

First of all, Luther recognized, as do all those who understand this problem, that at best a rational approach to the knowledge of God can never go beyond a high degree of probability. But to Luther the commonly accepted rule, "Probability is the guide of life," would have been an abomination in the area of religious knowledge. Luther says that the very essence of unbelief is that men say, "I do not know. I am not sure."[88]

Faith is a God-created certainty and assurance. He says,

> Properly speaking, faith is that which endures
> in extreme evils and holds fast to the Word of
> life and in this way conquers all the might of
> the devil, all terrors and all dangers, through
> which it enters with glory and confidence
> into eternal life.[89]

Even the most ardent defenders of natural theology will generally agree that such a firm and settled assurance cannot be found in natural theology.

Luther saw that natural theology can maintain itself only with the greatest difficulty. Long before the antinomies of Kant were announced to the world, Luther had already laid down the rule:

> No reason is so firm that it can not again be
> overthrown by reason. There is no counsel, no
> matter how wise, no thing, no edifice, no mat-
> ter how magnificent or strong, which cannot

again be destroyed by human counsel, wisdom, and strength. And this can be seen in all
things. Only the Word of God remains to all
eternity (*Solum verbum Dei in aeternum manet*).[90]

Many of those who set great store by natural theology do so
only because they are satisfied with "a high degree of probability."[91] This viewpoint is expressed by L. H. DeWolf in his
book, *The Religious Revolt Against Reason*, where he writes,

It must be freely admitted that absolute certainty, regarding most matters of importance
at least, is beyond the reach of human reason.
It should be added that it is beyond the reach
of man, whatever instrument he may choose
for its attainment.[92]

Luther would have agreed wholeheartedly with the first
sentence. He would have disagreed vehemently with the
second. To Luther all doubt in matters pertaining to God is
sin.[93] Precisely because he rejected "probability" as the enemy
of faith, he considered the natural knowledge of God to be of
limited value. "The right faith," he says, "is complete trust of
the heart in Christ."[94]

But the natural knowledge of God is by its very nature subject
to doubt, and human reason can never come to a sure knowledge (*gewis erkendnis*) of God.[95] But *sure knowledge* is what we
must have, if we are to have peace of conscience. This, to
Luther, was always basic to the whole problem.

It is just at this point that Luther parts company with
neo-orthodoxy and its emphasis on the unreliability of the
natural "proofs." Up to this point there is a certain similarity
between Luther's thought and that of Kierkegaard, although,
so far as I know, Luther never said that the proofs were
"harmful" to faith, as Kierkegaard did.[96] But the new fashion

in theology has reduced all religious knowledge to the level of natural theology, at least so far as intellectual certainty is concerned. Emil Brunner, for example, says that when the church seeks for certainties she is doing something that always turns out to be disastrous.[97] For that reason he opposes the concept of divinely inspired, and therefore "infallible," doctrine.[98] He calls upon the church to recognize the "element of untruth which clings to every human formulation of divine truth" and the fact "that in our hands the divine revelation is always mingled with error and arrogance."[99]

For Luther the doctrines of faith were infallible and certain. He would have criticized the spirit of intellectual doubt and uncertainty that neo-orthodoxy has introduced into the church much more severely than he criticized the vacillations of Cicero and the heathen.

Luther saw that the conclusions of reason in the area of natural theology could not be certain because there are elements in human experience that speak against those conclusions. The factor in human experience which is especially responsible for the failure of human reason to maintain even the barest elementary knowledge of God with abiding conviction is the evil that we observe in the world.

In a comment on Psalm 129:4, Luther writes that it is necessary that the Word assure us that God is just, because when we look at the way the world is governed, God seems to be completely unjust. He favors the godless with wealth and prosperity and power, and the heretics win fame and the approval of the populace. To be God is to be omnipotent. But an omnipotent God must be able to prevent wickedness, or, if it is already in existence, to destroy it. To be God is to be omniscient, and as such God must know what is happening in our world. To be God is also to be perfectly good, and as such God ought to want no evil to exist. If God is omnipotent, omniscient, and perfectly good and just, he is able, he knows

how, and he wants, to oppose evil. The existence of evil, therefore, is a living testimony against God. "This argument of
Epicurus and people like him," says Luther, "is plainly unan-
swerable."[100] He continues,

> Moreover, these things which in themselves
> are difficult for intelligent men, Satan makes
> even more difficult. For because we are forced
> to ascribe to God omnipotence, wisdom, and
> goodness, the devil, from the premises that
> we have granted, argues against us; and this
> very thing, which we are forced to ascribe to
> God, Satan again tears out of our hands, as it
> were, so that, overcome by the government of
> present affairs, we hold that either there is no
> God or that he is weak and helpless. Thus
> Aristotle comes wholly to this conclusion,
> that, even if he does not call God shameful,
> yet he lets God be ignorant of all things, so
> that God knows and sees none of our affairs,
> and thinks of nothing except himself and
> delights in nothing but the contemplation of
> his own Being. . . . But what kind of God is
> this, and what good is he to us?[101]

Luther goes on to say the Holy Ghost diverts us from this
stumbling-block when he assures us in the Word that God is
just. We are not to judge by what we experience in the present,
but only to believe what God tells us about the future.[102]

When Luther here in his own words repeats the argument of
Epicurus, he plainly indicates that this is a very natural
conclusion of the very same reason which has from other
evidence concluded that there is a God. In another place
Luther says that God has a habit of giving the very best
things to the worst of men, so that he permits the Sodomites
to live in a veritable paradise. This, he says, is a very grave

offense which tries even the patience of the saints, to say
nothing at all about the wise men of this world and the
philosophers.[103] And if those who have the Word and the
promises of God are scarcely able to resist this temptation,
how can we expect the wise men of this world, whose knowledge of God is based on philosophy, to maintain any kind of
sure knowledge? This offense, according to Luther, reason
will never be able to overcome.[104]

Earlier we took note of Luther's words in which he praises
Cicero's treatment of the subject of natural theology. In that
same connection Luther also criticizes Cicero, for even
though Cicero had dealt with the proofs for the existence of
God in a very commendable way and had come to correct
conclusions regarding it,

> yet, even though he comes to this conclu-
> sion, nevertheless he is overwhelmed by the
> vacillations of his speculations, so that at
> times this opinion is not firmly held and it
> seems to slip through his fingers. For this
> argument about infinity is so strong, that
> the place of religion is again torn out of our
> reason when we see this natural world over-
> whelmed by various calamities.[105]

This doubt, which flows out of rational considerations, at its
worst begins to question not only the justice of God but even
his very existence. And at its best, when it dares to deny
neither his justice nor his existence, and when it considers
God to be good, gracious, merciful, and kind—even when it
believes that God can help and that he knows how to help—
it still cannot believe and be sure that he is willing to do this.
Reason, Luther holds, can never attain to the stability of
faith. Reason believes and knows that God is almighty, but it
has doubts about the will of God to help, for in times of
trouble it experiences the very opposite and becomes

convinced that God does not want to help.[106] This is evidently what Luther meant when he said that the conclusions of reason are weak.[107]

It ought to be apparent to everyone who has read Luther carefully that he does not reject natural theology out of hand and that he places some value on the so-called "proofs." One of his chief reasons for downgrading natural theology is that it is unable to give full certainty. And it bears repeated emphasis that it is just here that Luther and neo-orthodoxy can never be brought to terms with each other. Luther believed that the propositional revelation given in the Word is absolutely true and that the statements of Scripture could give men a sure knowledge of God. It is far superior to any conclusions reached on rational grounds, for these can always be attacked on rational grounds.

For Luther and for anyone to whom the greatest question in life is "How can I find a gracious God?" and whose sense of sin is overpowering, so that he cannot have any real peace of mind until he has found the certainty of forgiveness, such unstable knowledge of God is of little use. Luther saw no profit in knowing God as Aristotle knew him, as "a being separate from his creatures and contemplating his creatures within himself," and so he asks, "What is that to us?" The God who is known to reason on rational grounds Luther calls a philosophical, Aristotelian God, and he says of this God, "He means nothing to us"[108] (*Nihil vero est ad nos*). To a long and learned defense of the existence of God based on rational arguments, Luther might well have answered, "Yes, yes, brother, but what of it? Even if we could prove beyond question that there is a God, we would still not know what we need to know."

Luther did not disparage the natural knowledge of God because it was rational, but because it was unstable and incomplete.

A TWOFOLD KNOWLEDGE OF GOD

Luther also has other reasons for laying little stress on natural revelation. He distinguishes sharply between two kinds of knowledge of God, and the distinction he commonly makes is not the one we usually make today when we speak of natural knowledge and revealed knowledge. To Luther both kinds of knowledge were forms of revealed knowledge.

In Romans I St. Paul says that the heathen know God. St. John makes the assertion that no man has seen God. And again, Jesus told the Pharisees that they did not know God. Commenting on these facts, Luther asks, "How can this be made to agree?" [109]

He answers his own question by saying that there is a twofold knowledge of God. The one is a knowledge of the law and the other is the knowledge of the gospel. The knowledge that comes out of the law is known to reason. But it is not the right knowledge of God, whether it comes from Moses or from the innate capacity of our heart. The right kind of knowledge is that which comes from the gospel, according to which we know that we are saved from sin, death and the devil by the incarnation, death and resurrection of God's Son. [110] He writes,

> The evangelical knowledge of God . . . does not grow in our garden. Reason knows not a drop of it . . . and it is hidden from her. She speaks of it as a blind man speaks of colors. The first way of knowing God is natural and common, and it is renewed through the law of Moses. But the evangelical knowledge must be preached from above and formed into the heart—that is, one must learn that God gives grace and truth through his beloved Son. Therefore, see how blind the world is in this second way of knowing God. [111]

It is rather surprising to hear Luther say that the right knowledge of God does not come from Moses. At first glance this seems to imply that the writings of Moses are not an authoritative message from God. There can be no doubt that Luther believed that Moses was an inspired spokesman of God. How then are we to reconcile this with Luther's disparaging statement about the law of Moses?

In the first place, the context makes it clear that Luther was thinking only of a knowledge of the law. What he is saying is that even if we have as complete a knowledge of God as it is possible to acquire from the law, we still will not know God as he wants us to know him.

This remark, therefore, is also of great significance for our understanding of Luther's concept of natural revelation. The natural knowledge of God is so limited and inadequate that in the matter of salvation it is equivalent to total ignorance.

In his commentary on Galatians he raises the same question in these words, "If all men know God, then why does Paul say that the Galatians had not known God before he preached to them?" Once more Luther answers that there is a twofold knowledge of God, but this time he distinguishes between a general knowledge (*cognitio generalis*) and a special knowledge (*cognitio propria*). The first belongs to all men, and according to it they know that there is a God, that he is the Creator of heaven and earth, and that he is the just Judge of all men. The special knowledge of God consists in this that we know "what God's thoughts are towards us, what he wishes to give and do that we might be freed from sin and death and be saved." This knowledge men do not have by nature.[112]

Without this special knowledge of God, men remain blind in spiritual things. The natural knowledge of God is "a useless, empty knowledge, if it stands by itself (*so es allein ist*)."[113] The

qualifying phrase is important, even if Luther sometimes
seems to say that this knowledge is not really knowledge at all.
In the same connection Luther writes,

> To know God's will does not mean that one
> only knows how to talk about him as the Jews
> and the Mohammedans do, that he has created
> heaven and earth and has given the law.[114]

The heathen, who "feel God" when they see his works, Luther
says, do not really know God, for they believe not with a theological but with a human reason (*non ratione theologica sed
humana*).[115]

In a lecture on Deuteronomy 4:3,4, delivered in 1524, Luther
refers to the first chapter of Romans once again and says that
the heathen "know God," but then he continues,

> Therefore, where there is no word of God,
> there is no true knowledge of God. Where
> there is no knowledge of God, there one will
> find only ungodly ignorance, imagination,
> and opinions about the true God as though
> he were pleased with what we choose for our-
> selves. But these are all ungodly services
> which do not bring us into contact with the
> true God (*quibus deus verus non tangitur*), but
> only with imaginations and images (*phantas-
> mata et idola*) of our own heart.[116]

The Mohammedans, the Jews, and all non-Christians claim to
know God, according to Luther, but their knowledge is
nothing more than the useless thoughts of blind, foolish
people—ideas with which the devil deceives and bewitches
them so that they think they have the true God.[117] The knowledge a man can gain from rational conclusions based on purely
rational premises (*vernunfftigen ursachen*) is far too limited to be

of any real value for the man who is concerned with the question of salvation.[118] Even the most excellent discussions of the pagan philosophers on the subject completely ignore the sending of God's Son for the salvation of sinners, and even their most excellent opinions about God are the deepest ignorance of God and mere blasphemies.[119]

It is very evident from these words that when Luther spoke of the ignorance of natural man in divine things, he did not mean to say that man by nature has no knowledge of God at all, nor that he was unable to discover anything about God by the use of his reason. We shall perhaps be able better to understand Luther's thoughts in this matter if we call to mind his comment on Isaiah 40:7, in which he says that the glory of man—not only his sins, his adulteries, his thefts—but also his good works and his deeds of mercy are destined for the fire.[120] In the same vein he says that the "best thoughts" of the heathen about God and his will are worse than Cimmerian darkness.[121] The "badness" does not consist in this that every thought is positively incorrect, but in the fact that even an occasional "correct thought" is condemned to drown in the endless sea of ignorance which surrounds it.

In seeking an understanding of Luther's position in this matter, it is necessary also to remember that for Luther the important question is never this: "Is there a God?" To ask that question, for Luther, constitutes the kind of blasphemy of which no honest man would make himself guilty. What man needs rather is an answer to the question, "Is God my God? Does he love me? Does he care for me?" Luther writes,

> Therefore it is not enough, and cannot be called a worship of the true God, if we worship him as the Mohammedans and Jews and the whole world without God's Word and faith boast—that they worship the only God, who made heaven and earth, and so forth. Up to

that point you have come to know neither his
divine essence nor his will. That there is a God,
by whom all things were made, that you know
from his works, . . . but God himself, who he
is, what sort of divine Being he is, and how he
is disposed toward you—this you can never
discover nor experience from the outside *(das
kanstu nicht von auswendig ersehen noch erfaren).*[122]

The distinction that Luther makes here finds concrete expression when he draws a sharp contrast between the knowledge
of God that one finds in Plato and that possessed by Joseph.
Of Plato's knowledge he says,

The philosophers dispute and inquire about
God by speculation, and they come to a kind
of knowledge. In this way Plato saw and recognized the principle of divine government.
But everything is considered so objectively
that it is not yet the kind of knowledge that
Joseph had, namely, that God cares for, hears,
and helps those who are afflicted. This is
something Plato was not able to assert. He
never gets beyond a metaphysical frame of
mind, like a cow staring at a new gate.[123]

Here we have the principle which Kierkegaard reiterated *ad
nauseam,* but in a much more abstract and abstruse fashion,
namely, that true knowledge of God must be subjective. We
know God truly only when we know him as he has revealed
himself to us in his Word. There, as Luther says, he clearly
proclaims himself to be "my Lord and God, and he
commands me to accept this in faith, for there a sure and firm
foundation is laid on which souls may rest." [124] This is the
knowledge that Joseph had and Plato lacked. When Joseph
was sold and falsely accused and unjustly imprisoned, he could
still say, according to Luther,

> I see that this is the will of God, who with-
> out doubt has something greater and more
> sublime in mind than I am now able to
> understand. Of this I am certain, that he will
> not desert me nor reject me. His will is
> incomprehensible, but still best, and I have no
> doubt that he wants to and is able to deliver
> me from these evils. . . . God will not leave
> me. What he plans for me, I do not rightly
> know. . . . But I know that he has better things
> in mind than I know now. I know that his will
> is well-disposed toward me. Therefore I com-
> mend myself to the Lord my God, who alone
> is wise and powerful and good.[125]

This is the right way to know God. "To know," for Luther
meant to enter into a personal, subjective relationship with the
object or person known.

Plato's knowledge, then, is not true knowledge, but not
because it is positively in error. What he knows is true as far
as it goes, but his knowledge is false because he does not know
God subjectively, nor does he know Christ. But Luther goes
even farther than this. A man may believe not only that God
made all things, but also that Christ was born of a virgin, that
he suffered, died, and rose again—and still have no true
knowledge of God.[126]

> This is true knowledge, that you believe and
> know that God and Christ are your God and
> your Christ. This the devil and the false
> Christians cannot believe. So the true knowl-
> edge of God is nothing else but the Christian
> faith. For when you know God and Christ in
> this way, then you will also with your whole
> heart rely on him and trust him in adversity
> and prosperity, in life and in death.[127]

We will not be able to understand Luther's thought correctly unless we bear in mind his definition of the knowledge of God and the sharp distinction which he makes between a philosophical, or metaphysical, knowledge of God and the true and proper knowledge of God. Because of his flair for unusual, startling expressions, which is really part of his creativity as a master of language, Luther, more than most writers, must always be read in wide context. By making a judicious selection of isolated statements, it is easy to turn Luther into a follower either of Barth or of Butler. Only a wide acquaintance with Luther's writings can guard us against both extremes. It is not surprising, for example, that Emil Brunner began his career with the confident conviction that Luther and he saw eye to eye, but upon closer acquaintance with the writings of the great reformer he became convinced that Luther is traditionally orthodox and not neo-orthodox.[128] It is likewise clearly evident from a careful examination of Luther's own words, that those who claim he rejected the natural knowledge of God as valueless are either ignorant of the facts or deliberately concealing them.

LUTHER'S REJECTION OF THOMISM

While Luther did not utterly depreciate the value of natural theology neither did he give it the exalted place it had occupied in the scholastic thought of Thomas Aquinas. In fact, Luther's thoroughgoing rejection of Thomism constitutes an additional reason for his seeming lack of appreciation for natural theology.

Luther has been quoted as saying, "I firmly believe that those who think that philosophy and the natural knowledge are useless in theology err greatly." This remark, dated in 1521, is believed by the editors of the Weimar Edition of his works to be very likely not genuine.[129] Yet it seems that Luther could have said something like this, because it is evident from what we have already seen that Luther did believe that natural theology had some validity and force. What Luther did not believe is that reason and natural theology could do what Aquinas believed it could do. Luther consistently held instead that natural theology is always uncertain, inadequate, misleading and legalistic.

Luther condemns the whole scholastic concept of the place of natural theology. He sees a conflict between natural knowledge—at least, in the use that is made of natural knowledge by the depraved reason of man—and the true knowledge of God. He writes,

> Where Christ is absent, there is darkness, no matter how great and bright it may appear to be. This leaves no room for an intermediate state, invented by the scholastics, who say that between the darkness and Christ there is the natural light and human reason. Thus they ascribe darkness only to manifestly bad men and fools. But the intermediate light they consider to be good, and they say that it may be well suited to the light of Christ. They agree that it is darkness compared to the light of Christ, but in itself it is a light. They, however, do not see, although they consider themselves to be enlightened in rich measure, that generally the most wicked are the most rational and the children of this world wiser in their ways than the children of light, as Christ says, and yet they are no better equipped for the true light than all the others. That would not happen if this light promoted the true light. Also, the devils are more clever, more rational (*vornunfftiger*), and wiser than all men, but they are no better on that account. Yes, it is a light that is always inimical to the true light.[130]

The scholastic theologians, following Thomas, had held that
if a man follows the dictates of reason in religion, he could
come to a recognition of the necessity of revelation, and when
on this road he had reached the point where he was ready to
accept guidance, God would not fail to give him the aid that
was necessary to bring him to a fuller knowledge of God.
Luther, however, says that the dictum of the scholastics,
"When a man does what he can, God will unfailingly give
grace" (*Homo cum facit, quod est in se, Deus infallibiliter dat gratiam*),
is disproved by the example of the philosophers. "Cicero,"
Luther says, "did what was in him," he did what he could, and
in his books, *"de natura deorum"* and *"de finibus,"* "he omitted
nothing that can be done by a man through human reason
and all his powers."[131] In spite of this, he did not obtain
grace, but instead fell into deeper darkness so that finally he
began to have doubts about the very existence of God. So,
Luther writes,

> It happens inevitably that he who thinks
> about these things without the Word, relying
> only on the light of reason, must err more
> and more.[132]

It is simply impossible, he says, in another place, for human
reason to lead us aright, and those who follow it must go
astray.[133]

Because of this, the natural knowledge of God is far from
being the first step in the journey that leads to a full and true
knowledge of God. Instead, its natural and inevitable consequence is the sin of idolatry. The worship of Jupiter and Mars
is a direct result of the fact that men have a natural knowledge
of God. In one of his sermons in Wittenberg, Luther told his
congregation, "So reason must make idols and it cannot do
otherwise."[134] At another time he said,

> From the fact that all men hold this major
> premise, "There is a God," all idolatry is
> born. Without a knowledge of God there
> would have been no idolatry in the world.
> Indeed, because men had this natural knowl-
> edge of God, they conceived, outside of and
> against the Word, vain and ungodly ideas
> about God.[135]

In the commentary on Jonah, to which we have already alluded
several times, he wrote,

> So reason plays the part of a blind cow with
> God and makes nothing but mistakes. It
> always misses the mark and gives the name of
> God to that which is not God. Reason would
> not do any of these things if it were unaware
> of God's existence, or if it knew who or what
> God is.[136]

In these words there breathes a spirit which could never be
reconciled with the Thomistic view, which held that reason
where it is not misled by man's lower faculties always has at
least a tendency to go in the right direction. The man who
took this position could never give to natural theology the seat
of honor that it enjoys in Roman dogmatics and in many
Protestant circles.

Yet, from such statements of Luther we must not conclude
that he held the natural knowledge to be valueless. If the only
quotations we could make from Luther were like the above, we
would probably have to agree that the Weimar editors are
correct—that Luther never said it was wrong to consider the
natural knowledge of God to be without value.

But there are many places where Luther expresses a high regard
for the "proofs" of God's existence, even while, on the other

hand, he disparages the Thomistic evaluation of the natural knowledge of God. To resolve this apparent contradiction, we have to bear in mind Luther's biblical view of the depravity of man. The corruption of human nature is so radical that it spoils everything it touches. Natural theology ends in idolatry, not because of some inherent weakness in the natural revelation of God, but because of the evil inclination of the human heart. Fallen mankind abuses all of the good gifts of God, including the gift of human reason—that most excellent gift for which Luther thanks God in his explanation of the First Article.

NATURAL KNOWLEDGE ALWAYS LEGALISTIC

A final reason, and perhaps the most important reason, for Luther's position on this subject grows out of his own spiritual and theological development. Brought up in an atmosphere of strict and severe discipline, reared in the legalism of the Roman Church, and steeped in the monastic ideals of righteousness, Luther developed an overpowering sense of sin. The "righteousness of God" was a phrase that filled him with fear. When in 1519 he finally came to a clear understanding of the doctrine of justification by faith, he saw that the way of salvation cannot be found in the law.[137] The law, by itself, must lead men either to pride and presumption or to despair.

But the natural knowledge of God is always a *cognitio legalis,* a law knowledge. We have already noted, in discussing the so-called "moral proof" for the existence of God, that Luther says a man knows what is right and wrong by nature. He has high words of praise for the legal enactments of the heathen. "The Romans [i.e., the ancient heathen Romans] laid down the very finest statutes and laws."[138] If Luther were not such a reliable theologian otherwise, we would almost feel like disagreeing with him when we hear him say,

> They [the heathen Romans] know better how
> to govern external things than St. Paul and
> other saints. Therefore the Romans also had

glorious laws and statutes. For reason told
them that murderers should be punished,
that thieves should be hanged, and how
inheritances should be distributed. All this
they knew and did in a splendid and orderly
way without any counsel or instruction from
the Holy Scriptures or the apostles. . . .
Although it was a godless kingdom and per-
secuted the Christians bitterly, yet they ruled
by reason and were respected by everyone.
They kept the peace. At their time there was
peace, and the world was open. This was an
earthly, rational government.[139]

Luther spoke also of the virtues of the heathen, and of
outstanding examples of continence, generosity, patriotism,
parental and filial love, courage, and kindness found among
them.[140] He actually preferred heathen authors over the
scholastic theologians for the study of morals. He maintained
that if all we need is to be told what is honest, beautiful and
good, we need none of the writings of the scholastics. Cato
and Aesop and Cicero, and even the hated Aristotle, are better
teachers of morals than the scholastic theologians.[141] Of the
pagan philosophers he said, "As far as their moral precepts are
concerned, one can find no fault with the industry and the
diligence of the heathen."[142]

He recognized that from a sociological and political point of
view the works and attitudes of the heathen might be called
good. But from a theological point of view a man without the
Holy Spirit is wicked, even if he is adorned with all virtue.[143]
Against the argument that reason is able to effect the most
beautiful virtues and therefore cannot be under the devil,
Luther says that the devil rules even in the best of our
virtues.[144] All the most admirable and most useful things in the
world are damned by God.[145] Even when a man's domestic and

political righteousness is as perfect as can be, he must still say, "Have mercy on me, O God. . . . Against you, you only, have I sinned." [146]

Moreover, this knowledge of the law, excellent as it may be in itself, often leads men to pride and presumption. Coupled inextricably with this knowledge of the law is a legalistic concept of salvation. Man naturally believes that he will be saved by "being good." A modern "philosophical defense of the Trinitarian-theistic faith" [147] defends the righteousness of God by saying, "God's nature, then, is one which expresses itself in making the kind of world where some men go to heaven for obedience and some go to hell for disobedience." [148] It is precisely this sort of theology that Luther rejects. "What good does it do you," he asks, "if all you can say is that God is gracious to the pious and punishes the wicked?" [149]

Work-righteousness is an inborn attitude of man. Reason knows only the religion of works. [150] Human reason is not able to free itself from the habitual and permanent opinion that man's righteousness is an active, personal uprightness, rather than the passive righteousness bestowed freely for Christ's sake, proclaimed in the gospel, and accepted by faith. This is one of the evils engrafted in human nature. [151] Luther says,

> This pernicious opinion about the law, that it justifies, sticks very tenaciously to reason, and by it the whole human race is held so securely that it can be freed from it only with difficulty. [152]

Human reason insists on making a tradesman out of God and says, "If I obey him, I will be in favor." In proud presumption reason seeks to strike a bargain with God and says, "If you will give, I will give." [153] In this opinion both monk and Mohammedan agree. Both of them think that if I do this or that work, God will be merciful to me; if I do not, he will be angry.[154] Of the men who opposed his reformation, Luther wrote,

> Look at their books and examine their doctrine diligently. Is it any more than a doctrine of works? "This is beautiful, this is honest," they say, "therefore do it!" "That is filthy and shameful, therefore avoid it!" And when they teach such things they imagine themselves to be true theologians and doctors.[155]

Man cannot free himself from such a *quid pro quo* (this in exchange for that) attitude in his relationship with God. It is part of his nature as a sinner. And in his blindness he even seeks to determine by his own will what will please God and move him to mercy. This point of view lies at the root of the whole monastic system. If there is any difference between the religion of the heathen and the religion of the monks, it is this, Luther says, that the work-righteousness of the monks is more wicked and more foolish than that of the heathen. The works of the heathen are at least in conformity with the law written in the heart. Luther writes,

> The barefoot monks have been much blinder than the heathen, for they have been of the opinion that if I would put on a gray cap, use a rope as a belt and make a vow of poverty, chastity, and obedience to the pope, I would please God well and I would not only be saved, but I could even share my good works with others. Where is that written? You will find that neither in Moses, nor in reason, nor in the gospel. They think that God sits in the heavens and tailors hoods, ropes, and sheets for the barefooted monks. It is the same

knowledge of God that the heathen had—
yes, Cato was superior to them.[156]

Speaking of his own life in the monastery, Luther said, "The
holier we were, the blinder we became and the more purely we
worshiped the devil."[157] The heathen were guilty of a similar sin.

> They made such a God for themselves who
> was worshiped by their own ideas and
> efforts, and so they glorified themselves as
> people who were able to do something pleas-
> ing to God by their own powers and to merit
> his grace. This is dishonoring God—not giv-
> ing thanks for what is received from him but
> being proud and presumptuous concerning
> what we offer to him. This is nothing else
> than a desire to have God made by us and
> not us by God, or to make the counsels and
> the thoughts of God similar to our counsels
> and thoughts.[158]

But while some men proudly boast of what they have done,
others are driven to despair.[159] For although men know what
is right, they have no power to do what is required by God
in the law. And because they do not meet the requirements,
it does them little good to know the law. "Nothing in us
follows his will," says Luther, and so the natural knowledge
of the law finally becomes "a damnable knowledge (ein
verdamlich erkentnis) of our own eternal destruction."[160] There
will be all too much of that knowledge when a man is overcome by fear or when he finds himself in danger of death.[161]
So it always remains useless, vain knowledge, which cannot
bring salvation, for by it a man knows and feels the wrath of
God all too well, and it becomes a very difficult and bitter
task for men again to unlearn this knowledge and to forget it
in the knowledge of Christ.[162]

To know God does not mean that through
reading I know his wisdom, omnipotence,
and all his miracles. For such knowledge
drives men to despair. But God is truly
known when he is known through Christ, and
by this knowledge all despair is driven out.[163]

THE VALUE OF NATURAL KNOWLEDGE

Still it would be a mistake, as we have noted earlier, to say that
Luther despised the natural knowledge of God. When Luther
calls this knowledge useless, he does so only in a particular
context. He means that it is theologically useless, that is, it
brings no sure and saving knowledge of God. But he did
believe that it was of great value for the maintenance of
outward order and discipline in the world. He writes,

The heathen people are endowed, not only
with reason and wisdom, but also with a free
will by which they conform to an honorable
and outwardly holy life. For if that had not in
some way been put in man's power, how could
discipline be maintained and laws enacted?
That some, however, permit their evil desires
to be restrained by the chains of the law, . . .
who does not see that this is a work of
human reason, which it is able to do by itself
alone, without the Holy Spirit.[164]

Nevertheless we must be careful to keep in mind, he says, that
while reason is able to guide men in living an outwardly decent
life, yet it is useless as far as the remission of sins and eternal
life is concerned.[165] Christ wants us to seek salvation and
forgiveness only in him. On the other hand,

He wants men to use the light of reason and
their moral powers or will for the government
of the affairs of this world and for maintaining

> an honorable outward life. For both of these
> this reason and will are adequate.[166]

It is evident that Luther would have little patience with those
theologians who recoil at the thought of the "awful punishment" the government metes out to murderers and rapists.

And this is not the only value to be found in the natural
knowledge of God and his will. Luther believed that it was
important, not as a point of departure, as in Thomism, but as
a point of contact in the proclamation of the biblical revelation of God. We might say that it has pedagogical, if not theological, value. He says that if the natural knowledge of the law
were not written in man's heart, we would have to preach for a
long time before the conscience of men would be pricked.
When the law is preached, the heart of man tells him that
these things are true and right and good. "Of that one could
not so soon convince him if it had not been previously written
in the heart," he wrote.[167]

REASON'S INCOMPETENCE IN THE AREA
OF SCIENTIFIC KNOWLEDGE

Modern neo-orthodox Lutherans often insist that Luther's
view of the natural knowledge of God justifies their saying
that reason is incompetent to judge divine matters but that in
the area of history, geography, science, and other secular
matters reason must be allowed to rule. The theological
truths of the Bible, therefore, are to be accepted in faith, but
in all other matters the statements of Scripture are subject to
the same kind of rational criticism that would apply to any
other book.

But those who hail as significant Luther's disparagement of
reason in the area of theology, ought not to overlook another
aspect of Luther's concept of man's natural knowledge of
divine things. Up to this point we have seen that man,

according to Luther, has no true knowledge of God and no
true knowledge of the law. But Luther goes much farther than
this. Four hundred years before Van Til, Luther held that man
can have no true knowledge of anything at all in creation by
the powers of reason. If this is true, then surely Luther's statement that man can have no true knowledge of God must be
seen in a new light.

Luther did not deny that reason could discover many things
(this we shall treat in another place), but he did hold that
natural reason, which does not know God, is also ignorant of
that which has been created by God *(ignorat creaturam Dei)*.[168]
No one can understand a single work of God fully by the use
of reason. This a man will recognize to a certain extent, says
Luther, if he will only propose to himself the question of the
usefulness of straw.[169]

Luther did not condemn natural science, although he did
ridicule its pretensions to wisdom. He has some words of high
praise even for astrology, which he otherwise so vehemently
rejected. Stripped of its superstitions, it is not to be
condemned, for it is the observation and consideration of the
works of God, "which is the most worthy concern of man."[170]
Man can, in other words, find no better use of his talents than
the study of nature.

Natural science is therefore a legitimate interest of man, and
man may learn a great deal about nature through his own
experience, by instruction from others, and by divine revelation. But what man can learn in this way is only a small part
of nature. Furthermore, Luther adds,

> Since Adam's fall, by which reason was
> blinded, it is impossible to know nature
> beyond that which can be learned by experi-
> ence or divine enlightenment.[171]

And yet even in this limited area reason takes more delight in fables and lies than in the truth. As an illustration of the perversion of reason in natural science he points to the folly of astrology, which in Luther's day was widely accepted in scholarly circles, also by theologians, as a legitimate science. Even Melanchthon, for example, defended its validity.

Luther goes on then to ridicule Aristotle and his accomplishments in the area of natural science. He says,

> Here is that noble light of nature, the heathen master, the archmaster of all masters, who now rules and teaches in all the universities in the place of Christ—the highly renowned Aristotle! who has taught, and still teaches, that a stone is heavy, a feather is light, that water is wet, and fire is dry. . . . This is the skill of the universities. Whoever has learned this receives a brown hat and is called a worthy master of arts and philosophy. Whoever has not learned this skill, he is not able to be a theologian nor to understand the Holy Scriptures—yes, he must be a heretic and may not even be a Christian.[172]

Now, if human reason cannot deal adequately even with natural science, how can it hope to begin to solve questions about the origin and destiny of the world? Reason does not know the fact of creation. Aristotle wrestled with the problem and came to no sure knowledge, although he inclined toward the opinion that the world must be eternal. At least he insisted, says Luther, that one can neither posit a first nor a last man. Here human reason is forced to stop,[173] for it is just as absurd according to human reason to posit a beginning of the world as it is to assert its existence from eternity.[174]

In connection with this, Luther also asserts that man can have no true and sure knowledge of himself by the powers of reason. Man can never know himself adequately until he knows his fount, or origin, which is God.[175] In fact, rational, scientific evidence cannot even assure a man of his own origin in the first generation. I can only *believe* that I have this father and mother.[176] How much less, then, can reason inform us of ultimate origins! Without Moses it is impossible to know anything certain about the origin of man.[177] "This indeed is the wisdom of our reason, that we do not know our own origin if we do not have the Word."[178] Because of this, Luther set great store by the genealogies of Scripture, for they trace the line of man to its beginning. Those who do not have the Scriptures "do not know themselves, who they are or where they came from."[179]

Reason, however, considers the Biblical account of origins to be absurd. Luther said that if Aristotle were to read the account of Adam's creation, he would break out in laughter,[180] and if one were to follow reason, the story of the creation of Eve would sound like a fable.[181] Commenting on the account of Eve's creation, he writes, "Where will you find a man who would have believed this story of the creation of Eve, if it had not been so clearly handed down to us?"[182]

To know only present phenomena is to know scarcely anything. Luther asks, "For what . . . does a philosopher know about heaven and earth if he does not know where it comes from and where it is going? Yes, and what do we know about ourselves?"[183] It is very evident, then, that even if Luther were living in our present scientific age, he would not be greatly impressed by modern advances in science. After looking around, he would soon remind us that we have not yet discovered, by the scientific method, the answers to the important questions.

Moreover, without the Christian faith it is impossible to know any part of creation correctly. Luther says, for example, that one cannot know what a man is or what a woman is unless one is a believer. They are works of God, and the works of God just as much as the words of God can be known for what they are only by a believing child of God. We do not truly know our fellowmen unless we know them as creatures of God. It is for this reason that men are filled with unlawful sexual desire. If a man were to look at a woman and really know her as a creature of God, he would also know the proper use of the woman. All the miseries of married life arise, therefore, out of a lack of faith, because one spouse does not recognize the other as a creature of God.[184]

Scotus had defended the competence of human reason not only to know the creature but also to know God, for he set up the premise that a person who can love a lesser good is surely able to love also the greater good. He therefore held that since man can love the creature, he must be able also to love the Creator, who is certainly more worthy of love. Luther ridicules this approach. He says of it,

> A real theological conclusion, worthy of a doctor of darkness in the church! He does not see that a man, when he loves the creature most, loves it least as a creature. (For who ever loved a girl as a girl or gold as gold?) It is a love defiled by lust and avarice, and it can never be perfectly pure in this flesh.[185]

Here it is necessary to remember that for Luther anything that was not perfectly pure was damnable sin.

In his commentary on Genesis Luther says of the patriarchs,

> They had the knowledge of God. But whoever knows God also knows, understands and

> loves the creature, because the footsteps of
> God are in the creature. . . . The ungodly . . .
> know neither God nor his creatures, much
> less their proper use. . . . For the proper use
> of anything the Holy Spirit is necessary.[186]

These comments of Luther become very significant when we
see the concern modern science has about origins and values.
Luther would not have said that a proper scientific study of
this world should omit all reference to origins and values.
What he would have said is that science cannot operate properly if it ignores the revelation of God in Scripture. Science
may discover some "truth" but it can never put this truth to
proper use. There is hardly a better argument than this for
Christian education at all levels.

REASON'S INCOMPETENCE
FOR THE STUDY OF CAUSES

Luther approaches this whole problem of the knowledge of
our present visible world also from another point of view. He
says that the wisest of men do not know final and efficient
causes. In the modern scientific world final causes are usually
not considered at all. Hutchison quotes the remarks of
Francis Bacon, who said that final causes are like vestal virgins,
dedicated to the gods but unproductive, and, he continues,
"the Aristotelian classification that comes closest to modern
scientific views of cause is the efficient cause."[187]

Just at this point Luther would have raised violent protest. If
modern science agrees in Hutchison's estimate of its philosophy, it is deceiving itself. Luther would have said that just this
is the basic error of modern science—it professes to know
more than it knows. In reality it can find only material and
formal, or instrumental, causes, but in its ignorance it imagines that it has found efficient and final causes. It is this attitude which is behind the "scientific" assertion that diseases
cannot be caused by devils because they are caused by germs,

or that God cannot answer prayers for rain because rain is the result of the interacting of complicated meteorological factors. Man, with his reason, can only deal with phenomena, and he ought to be conscious of the limitations which this places on all his investigations. Reason has no way of pressing behind the phenomena to find the real efficient cause which controls and determines them. Man's metaphysical quest is therefore from the very outset doomed to disappointment, and the only purpose in studying philosophy is to find out that it does not have the answers we seek. Since reason cannot truly know God, and since God is the only true efficient cause, and God's will is the only true final cause, therefore reason can never go beyond material and instrumental causes. Consequently reason can never know anything correctly. Luther says,

> We see that we are men. But that we have this father or this mother—could we know this in any way if it did not behoove us to believe it? So all of our wisdom and knowledge is limited to a knowledge of material and formal causes, although even in this we are sometimes shamefully deceived. Efficient and final cause we plainly are not able to point out, which is especially burdensome when we must debate or think about the world in which we are and live, or about our own selves. Is this not a miserable and poor wisdom? Aristotle says, "Man and the sun generate men." What a wise saying that is! Follow this wisdom and you will find that you must hold that man and the sun are eternal and infinite. For you will never find a man who is either the first or the last, just as I am not able to find either the beginning or end of my own person if I want to know this with certainty and rather am not willing to believe it. But

what sort of wisdom, what sort of knowledge is this that knows neither efficient nor
final cause? We have a knowledge of form,
but in that way a cow knows her home; in
that way (as the German proverb has it), she
sees and recognizes the gate. Here you can see
how horrible is the fall into original sin, by
which we have lost this knowledge, so that
we are able to see neither our own beginning
nor end.[188]

Now we are ignorant, not only of our own origin and destiny,
but also of political and economic institutions. Men are able
by the use of reason to establish excellent governments and to
regulate political and economic life in a splendid fashion. But
even in this area the pagan philosophers (so Luther writes in
his commentary on Psalm 127)

knew only material and formal causes in politics and economics, but final and efficient
cause they did not know—that is, they did
not know where politics and economics come
from, by whom they are preserved, and for
what they are intended.[189]

Plato and Xenophon and Cicero and other ancient philosophers had much that was good to say in the field of political
and social life. But as soon as they began to speak of final and
efficient causes, they went astray. They knew no higher final
causes than political peace, honor, and fame, and they believed
that the good ruler and the good citizen were final causes. In
their views of material and formal causes they were correct.
"This cause they treated beautifully and well, but this is not
enough."[190] They were never able to go beyond this point, for
they had only reason to follow.[191] This is one of the great
differences between sociology, economics, and philosophy, on

the one hand, and theology, on the other. The former deal only with material and formal causes. The latter deals primarily with the efficient and final cause.[192]

It is evident that Luther believed that true knowledge of anything must be theological. Only in that light is it possible to understand Luther's disparagement of the natural knowledge of God.

CONCLUSION

In his whole treatment of natural theology, Luther is always intent upon this one thing: men must learn that sure and true knowledge of God can be found only in God's revelation. And God's certain revelation is to be found only in Scripture. Because of man's total depravity and blindness, he can never read the revelation of God in nature fully nor draw conclusions correctly and with certainty. God must come to our aid. Yet, because of man's weakness and sinfulness, the majesty of God must hide behind masks in order to reveal itself. Men should take care lest in sinful pride and presumption they are offended by the lowliness of the masks and by the simplicity of the Scriptures. It is the crib in which we find the Lord Jesus Christ. And only as we find him there, and God in him, can we know all creation correctly. "Therefore," Luther says,

> let us teach that true knowledge is found in Holy Scripture, in the Word of God. For it instructs us not only about matter, not only about the form of the whole creation, but also about the efficient and final cause and the beginning and end of all things, who has created it, and to what end he made it. Without knowledge of these two causes our wisdom differs little from that of beasts, who also use their eyes and ears, but clearly know nothing of a beginning or an end.[193]

CHAPTER III

REASON AS INSTRUMENT

John Wesley read Luther's commentary on Galatians, and he was surprised and repelled by Luther's attacks on human reason. Luther's denunciations of reason are often sharp and bitter, and many since Wesley's day have read Luther with the same feeling. For if reason should be rejected lock, stock, and barrel, as Luther's words often seem to imply, then what is the point in books like Luther's commentary on Galatians, or any book for that matter? "What is reason," asked Wesley, "but the power of apprehending, judging, and discoursing?"[1] And finally, as many have pointed out, the critics of reason must employ the very instrument which they depreciate; without it they would not be able to meditate on or discourse about the problem that they are attempting to solve.

REASON, A GREAT GIFT OF GOD
When the charge of rampant antirationalism is leveled against Luther, however, it flows either out of an ignorance of what he said or out of a failure to understand Luther's thought. It is, in fact, so difficult to misunderstand Luther's position that one can only conclude that those who do find fault with him on this score have not really read him extensively.

It is also important to remember that scholastic theology had exalted reason to an almost divine status and had sought to use it as a means for searching out the secrets of God. When Luther criticized reason, he often had in mind the speculative thought of scholasticism and the rationalistic approach to Scripture. (The next chapter will deal more thoroughly with this aspect of Luther's thought.)

But insofar as it is the instrument which man uses to examine his environment, to interpret his experiences and to discourse about them, Luther valued reason highly. The course that his thinking on this matter would take ought to be clear to anyone who knows his explanation of the First Article in the *Small Catechism*—where he lists "reason and all our faculties" among the Creator's gifts for which we ought to be grateful.

Luther often spoke of reason as a gift of the Lord which man ought not to depreciate. Toward the end of 1543 he lectured at Wittenberg on the ninth chapter of Isaiah. In the course of these lectures he said,

> Reason is a very great gift of God. Its value cannot be measured, and those things which it wisely ordains and discovers in human affairs are not to be despised.[2]

Earlier in the same lecture he had compared the light of reason to that of the sun:

> Who would not recognize that these lights are splendid? Who would despise them? . . . As, however, the light of the sun is splendid and admirable, so also is the light of reason, and indeed reason is a far more splendid light than that of the sun. . . . Reason can do what the sun cannot.[3]

We have already heard some of the complimentary things that Luther had to say about reason. And there are many remarks of this kind in his writings.

"Reason is a glorious light," he said at another time.[4] An *"egregrium lumen,"* he called it—"glorious" is almost too weak a translation for *"egregrium."* To say that it is a "splendid, magnificent" light would be more in keeping with the original. But at the same time, remember that he immediately added, "So is a wax candle—but what if the sun should rise?"[5] In a debate at Wittenberg in 1536 he said that reason even after the Fall (*post peccatum*) is still a very beautiful and a very excellent thing.[6] In one lecture he called it "a most outstanding gift."[7]

In 1536 Luther wrote a series of theses on the nature of man for a disputation at the University at Wittenberg. The fourth thesis reads, "It is certainly true that reason is the best thing of all, the chief thing, the best thing above all other things of this life, and something divine (*et divinum quiddam*)." He describes reason there as the inventor and governor of all arts, of medicine, and law, and whatever of wisdom and power and virtue and glory is possessed by man in this life. It is the chief part of man, and it constitutes the essential difference between men and animals. Significantly, in the course of the debate, Luther said, "And after the fall of Adam God did not take this majesty away from reason, but rather he confirmed it."[8]

Not only did Luther insist that the Fall had not destroyed the capacity of reason to examine and to interpret the data of experience furnished by the senses, but he held also that in conversion this aspect of our rational nature remains essentially unchanged. Luther specifically excluded reason, as such, from his definition of the image of God. He argued that the devil, who certainly does not have the image of God, has a better reason than men.[9] He pointed out that Jethro, whom he calls a heathen, taught Moses, a man who was completely filled with the Holy Ghost, how to rule. It was in this connection that Luther wrote, "The heathen have demonstrated far greater wisdom than Christians."[10] It would appear, then, that at least in this area, Luther gives more credit and honor to human reason than those do who criticize Luther for what they call his "irrationalism" and then proceed to include reason in the image of God, which has been obscured by the Fall.

Furthermore, according to Luther, even after conversion reason remains essentially unchanged. It is given a new spirit and a new direction in conversion, but its discursive and apprehending powers remain substantially unaltered. In the *Kirchenpostille*, which Luther considered to be one of his best publications, he is quoted as saying in a sermon,

> For although the gospel is a higher gift and wisdom than human reason, yet it does not alter or tear to pieces the understanding which God has implanted in human reason.[11]

THE SPHERE OF REASON

It must be said at this point that Luther sharply limits the sphere of reason when he speaks of it in this way, and yet we must be careful not to draw the lines of demarcation tighter than Luther himself draws them. Sometimes it seems as though Luther excludes reason completely from the realm of theology. But we shall see presently that he does not really do this.

Luther says, for example, "Reason, although it is beautiful and glorious, belongs only to the kingdom of this world. There it has its authority and its sphere *(Gebiete)*." [12] Reason has a place in governing this present world.[13] The things which belong to this temporal life and to the government of the world are subject to reason.[14] But the management of households and the ordering of the affairs of the common-wealth are the limits beyond which reason is not to go.[15] Reason and experience teach us how to rule wife and children, how to drive cows out to pasture and how to bring them in again.[16] It tells us that a pig must be handled differently from a cow, and that wine should not be made in a beer keg but in a wine barrel.[17]

> In outward and worldly things one ought to permit reason to exercise her judgment, for

there you are able to figure out things and to
understand that a cow is larger than a calf,
likewise, that three yards are longer than one
yard, that a dollar is more than a penny, that
a hundred dollars are more than ten dollars,
and that the roof is better situated on top of
the house than under the house. Stay with
those things. Such things are in your power.
With it you can well determine how to train
a horse. Such things reason teaches you.
There exercise your mastery, for God has also
given reason for this purpose that we should
milk cows and train horses.[18]

These words appear to be sarcasm, and when viewed from the
standpoint of scholastic theology, they were very likely
intended to be just that. But when we remember the high value
that Luther placed on the affairs of this life—he held that a
farmer who plows his field in fulfillment of his calling is
doing a greater work than a monk who spends all his time in
prayer without a call from God—we shall not surrender to the
temptation to interpret those words as an indication that
Luther placed a low value on reason, or that he considered it
useless for theological pursuits.

There is one other thing we should not forget. These statements do not deal with the exercise of reason in apprehending
or discussing religious truth, but rather with the ability of
reason to decide what is good and proper and beautiful and
right in this world. The common idea which runs through all
of these statements is contained in words like "authority,"
"management," "government," "ordering," "rule," "handling,"
"breaking," "training," and "mastery."

This evaluation of Luther's thought is further substantiated
by the fact that in the area of economics and government
Luther admired the accomplishments of the heathen, as we

have already noted in another context. He translated Aesop's fables for the schools of Germany because he considered them to be of great value for the education of the young. He delighted in the proverbs of the heathen. He spoke of "the excellent proverbs and teachings of the heathen authors."[19] He said that the heathen have made great contributions to the betterment of discipline and to the government of this world. To this history itself bears witness.[20]

Not to use reason in the sphere where God intended that it should be used is to tempt God.[21] There is no need to jump out of a window if there is a ladder available, nor does it make sense to walk through the Elbe when there is a bridge across the river. He writes in that connection,

> Nevertheless, God must not be tempted, that is, the means must not be neglected. But we must use the means which we are able to use, inasmuch as God has not given reason and the counsel and aid of reason that you should despise them.[22]

Thus it was perfectly proper for Abraham to go to Egypt during the famine even though he had no specific command of God to do this, "for in bodily perils reason has its place, so that it is able to see something and to give advice."[23] In regard to the efforts of Jacob to appease his brother Esau, Luther comments that in times of danger we must do what reason indicates.[24] In a similar vein he says that it was right for Noah to take food into the ark, for

> it is true that it is the will of God that all our works should be done in faith, but nevertheless it is not his will that we should neglect what lies at hand and he has previously given.[25]

THE PLACE OF REASON IN
COMMUNICATING RELIGIOUS TRUTH

But while the sphere of reason is this earthly life and this present world, yet Luther also has a place for reason in theology. It is true that he drastically limits its functions in this field. He was not willing to honor reason in any way as the source of any of the truths revealed in the gospel. Luther would never have subscribed to those views of revelation which reduce it to a process of discovery through the diligent use of reason on the basis of human experience. He also warned repeatedly against ever letting reason become the judge of Scripture. But he definitely held that reason has a place in theology as the instrument by which the truths of divine revelation are apprehended and understood.

There can be no doubt that at least in some respects Luther must be classified as an anti-metaphysical theologian. He definitely felt that philosophy had no positive contribution to make to theology. Casserley has pointed out that those who take an antirational stance in theology always run the risk of destroying the foundations on which the whole structure of language and all human communication is built.[26] They are forced to the conclusion that divine revelation cannot come to men through the medium of human speech—or, at least, that the revelation, when reduced to verbal, propositional form, always must become obscured and partially corrupted.

We have seen this very thing happen in neo-orthodoxy, where words have, in many instances, lost all concrete meaning, and theology has become what might almost be described as a form of impressionistic art.

Luther stood firm against this temptation. He would never have agreed with the man who said, "The study of logic is a curse to candidates for the ministry."[27] When he called for the reform of the German universities in his *Address to the German Nobility* in 1520, he asked that Aristotle's *Physics, Metaphysics, De Anima,* and

Ethics be dropped from the curriculum. But it is of the utmost significance here that Luther, even though he dubbed Aristotle "that damned, proud, rascally heathen," [28] nevertheless wanted to retain three of his works as text books for university study. They were Aristotle's *Logic, Rhetoric,* and *Poetry.* [29]

Significant also in this connection is the stress that Luther laid on the study of languages, especially Greek and Hebrew. In addition to the three works of Aristotle mentioned above, the core of the curriculum was to include mathematics, history, Latin, Hebrew, and Greek. [30] In 1524 Luther wrote his *Open Letter* to the members of the councils of all the German cities in which he called for the establishment of Christian schools, on both the elementary and the secondary level and for both boys and girls. In this letter he emphasized the need of training the youth of the nation in all the skills necessary for the welfare of the community. The greater emphasis, however, he laid on the study of language. He wrote,

> As dearly as we love the gospel, so diligently let us hold to the study of language. [The preceding context makes it clear that he had in mind especially Hebrew and Greek.] . . . And let us recognize that fact that we will not be able to preserve the gospel well without the languages. The languages are the scabbard in which this sword of the Spirit is sheathed. They are the jewel box in which we carry this treasure. They are the cask in which this beverage is contained. They are the pantry in which this food is kept. And as the gospel itself shows, they are the baskets in which these loaves and fish and fragments are preserved. [31]

He says further that if the study of Hebrew and Greek is neglected, the next step will be that interest in the languages in general will wane, and the time will come when men will be able to speak neither German nor Latin properly. He points to the example of the German universities and the monastic schools, where not only the gospel had been lost, but where men had become such rude beasts that they could neither speak nor write the common language correctly. They have, he says, almost lost even natural reason.[32] For a man who was ready to curse the universities because they had exalted reason, this last remark indicates most clearly that Luther understood the relation between communication and reason, and that he was therefore well aware of the danger pointed out by Casserley. The whole text of Luther's *Open Letter* is of great importance for a clear evaluation of his thought in this area, and we will return to it once more before we finish this chapter.

Philosophers and psychologists have at times attempted to draw a sharp line of demarcation between that function of the mind by which we "understand" and that by which we "reason."[33] It is questionable, however, that such a line can be drawn. Language is more than a complicated system of conditioned reflexes. This ought to be especially clear in theology, where it is often necessary to deal with abstractions. Unless we are willing to adopt the position of logical positivism, which rules such abstractions out of court, we have to recognize that "reasoning" and "understanding" are very closely related.

The same thing ought to be clear in the field of Bible interpretation, where it is necessary to exercise the capacities of the mind in what might be called linguistic judgment. Since a single word may have a half-dozen possible meanings, the interpretation of Scripture involves a procedure which we could classify as "problem solving" in every sense of the term. Luther recognizes the difference between so-called "primitive" understanding (such as men assume to be present also in animals) and the mental activity involved in hearing God's Word. He writes,

> One would have to preach to a donkey, a
> horse, an ox, or a cow for a hundred thousand
> years before they would accept the law,
> although they have ears and eyes and a heart,
> just as a man. They too can hear it, but it does
> not strike the heart. Why? What is lacking?
> The soul is not so formed and created that
> such things can strike it.[34]

So also on this score Luther cannot be called "irrationalistic." The modern participants in what has been called the neo-orthodox "revolt against reason" cannot claim him as their own.

Luther believed that it was possible for an unconverted man to understand the meaning of the Scriptures by the use of his natural powers of reason. This simply means that Luther expected no one to read the Scriptures in a cabalistic way. For him the Scriptures are not written in code. The revelation of God and the meaning that God wishes to convey to us through the words of Scripture are not hidden behind the words of the Bible. God may be hidden and, indeed, always remain hidden, but the Word through which the hidden God reveals himself is open to all. The revelation is there for all men, not only for those who somehow are initiated into the secret, or who have somehow become partakers of the "special" grace which modern followers of Calvinistic thought have renamed "personal encounter." No special enlightenment is necessary to know what the words of Scripture mean. The man who knows the language in which a word is written will know what the word intends to say to him. But to understand it, to grasp its meaning, to think about it, is not the same as to believe it.

In his *Open Letter* to the city councils Luther says that the fathers often erred in their teaching because they did not understand Hebrew or Greek. And even when they taught correctly, they often, on account of their ignorance of the languages, used proof texts which made them ridiculous in the eyes of the world, for the educated unbeliever could know that the text did not say what the fathers claimed to find in it.[35] In other words, an intelligent unbeliever understands the meaning of the Bible better than an ignorant but pious believer.

Luther said also that the scholastics' contention that the Bible is an unclear book is due to their ignorance of the languages.[36] The significance of this statement crystallizes when we contrast it with the explanation that is often given, namely, that the Scriptures are unclear to the unconverted because they have not been enlightened by the Holy Ghost. The "enlightenment" of the Holy Ghost, for Luther, did not have to do with the bare understanding of the meaning of the words of Scripture, but rather with the acceptance of those words in faith. The enlightened person in Luther's vocabulary was the believer in Jesus Christ. The believer, in approaching the Scriptures, uses his reason to "think about" the gospel. Luther says, "Reason serves faith in this way, that it thinks about these things." [37]

THE INTERPRETATION OF SCRIPTURE
The place of logical processes in Luther's theological thought comes into sharp focus when we examine the basic principles which underlie his whole approach to the interpretation of Scripture. It is well known that when Luther began his exegetical lectures at Wittenberg, he quickly turned away from the allegorical method, by which he said that Origen and Jerome had made fools of themselves.[38] Finally he abandoned the method almost entirely.

Today we see a disguised revival of the allegorical method in the tendency to reduce the Scriptural account to the level and status of mythology. But those who seek to claim Luther for neo-orthodoxy ought to keep in mind that Luther insisted on what he called the "historical literal meaning which is consistent with the text." [39]

An approach to Scripture which insists on this cannot be called irrational. And this was Luther's consistent exegetical method. He demanded that, in the interpretation of Scripture,

> the natural speech is the Kaiser's wife, and it
> is to be preferred to all subtle, sharp, and
> sophistic interpretations. One must not
> depart from it unless one is compelled to do
> so by a clear article of faith, or else not one
> letter of Scripture can be maintained against
> the spiritual jugglers.[40]

In the introduction to his Genesis lectures Luther indicates clearly what method he will follow. This world, of which Moses speaks, Luther holds, is no allegorical world. It is a real world, and these are real creatures, and (anticipating Darwin by three hundred years) the days of Genesis One are real days.[41]

Of the creation of Eve, in this same commentary, he says that we should forget all the foolish glosses of the scholastic commentators. He announces his resolution to treat the account as true history.[42] Again he makes special mention of the fact that he believes that Adam's rib was a real rib.[43] Scholastic theology had always allegorized the account of the Fall, at least in its theological significance, just as neo-orthodoxy mythologizes it away. But Luther urged his students to believe that the serpent was a real serpent, that the woman was a real woman, and that the man was a real man. He says, "According to this interpretation the serpent remains a serpent, but possessed by Satan, the woman remains a woman, and Adam remains Adam."[44]

In his answer to the Diatribe of Erasmus, he wrote,

> No conclusion or figure of speech is to be
> permitted in any Scripture passage, unless

the context clearly compels it and the absurdity of the matter manifestly conflicts with
an article of faith. Rather, everywhere we
must cling to the simple, pure, and natural
meaning of the words, which is dictated by
grammar and common usage, which God has
created in men.[45]

In these words to Erasmus we have an allusion to the second
great principle which Luther adopted in his exegesis, and this,
too, has significance for our thesis. The principle is that, in the
interpretation of the Bible, proper consideration should be
given to grammatical rules and to the context. In the *Tischreden*
Luther speaks of the rules that he gave to those who had
helped him in the work of translating the Bible. The third rule
that he lists there is "that one must pay attention to the
grammar."[46] Luther criticized Erasmus, who was recognized as
the most distinguished linguist of the day, because he did not
see that there is a real difference between the indicative and the
imperative mood. Erasmus had argued that from a command
of God ("Be holy, because I am holy!") it was possible to
conclude man's ability to fulfill that command.[47]

As the rules of grammar must receive proper consideration, so
the context must also be given due weight. In his Galatians
commentary Luther warned men against carrying their own
thoughts into Scripture,

since they ought to come empty and take all
their thoughts out of the sacred letters, then
diligently consider the words and compare
what precedes with what follows, and pay
attention to this: that they grasp the whole
sense of the passage and do not construct
their own dreams out of isolated words torn
out of context.[48]

In January of 1539 a disputation was held at Wittenberg on
the question whether the words, "The Word was made flesh,"
could be defended philosophically. In the course of this
debate one of the participants argued that dialectics, the
capacity for logical thinking, is a divinely given instrument
which is rightfully employed in the search for truth, and therefore it is to be used also in theology. Luther did not disagree
with this point of view, but he said that while it was to be
used, it should not be employed as mistress, but only as a
helper and slave and most beautiful servant, who teaches us
how to define and distinguish, but that beyond that point its
service must come to an end.[49]

SYLLOGISTIC ARGUMENTATION
IN DOCTRINAL THEOLOGY

While Luther insisted that all our premises in theology must
be taken from the Bible, he was not at all averse to the use of
formal logical processes in setting forth and demonstrating
the doctrines of the Christian faith. Here it would be possible
to heap up examples without number, but we shall restrict
ourselves to only a few illustrations of Luther's dogmatical
method in this regard.

Commenting on the statement in Hebrews 1, that God made
the world through his Son, he writes:

> If all is made through the Son, he himself
> must be uncreated. From this it follows clearly
> that he must be true God, for everything that
> is not made and yet is something must be
> God. . . . If he is a Son, he cannot be alone.
> He must have a Father. And if God made the
> world through him, then this God who made
> the world through him cannot be he through
> whom he made it. Thus it follows that there
> must be two persons, the Father and the Son,
> distinct from each other. And yet, since the

divine nature is one and there can be no more
than one God, it follows that Christ is one
God with the Father, in one divine essence,
one Creator and Maker of the world.[50]

Regularly, in dealing with the deity of Christ, Luther makes
use of the syllogistic argument. He sees the deity of Jesus in
many passages of Scripture that do not mention it specifically. In Matthew 23 the Lord Jesus says that he had sent
the prophets. Prophets are sent by God. Luther says,
"Therefore he is God."[51] Again, the angels of Bethlehem call
him Lord. If the angels call him Lord, he must be higher
than they. The only one higher than angels is God.
Therefore he is God.[52]

In 1530 Luther published an exposition of the seventeenth
chapter of John's Gospel. Commenting on the third verse,
"This is life eternal that they might know you, the only true
God, and Jesus Christ, whom you have sent," Luther says,

> There stand the clear, bare words, which
> every man can understand and grasp; Christ
> gives to all who believe eternal life. But since
> no one can give eternal life but God, therefore
> it follows incontrovertibly from this that
> Christ is true, natural God. Likewise, since he
> bases eternal life on this that one knows him
> and the Father, so that no one may attain to
> eternal life without a knowledge of him, so
> that it is one knowledge by which he and the
> Father are known, therefore he must be of
> one essence and nature with the Father, that
> is, the same true God, but a distinct person
> from the Father. This is so clearly and power-
> fully taught in this text, that even reason can-
> not contradict it.[53]

He employs the same sort of syllogistic reasoning in assuring
the Christian of his salvation. On the basis of the words,
"Behold the Lamb of God, who takes away the sin of the
world," he says in a sermon,

> Now you cannot deny that you are also a part
> of the world, for you were born of man and
> woman. You are not a cow or a pig, and there-
> fore your sins must also be included. . . .
> Everything which is called sin, world, and the
> world's sins, . . . all lies alone on the Lamb of
> God, and since you are also a part of the
> world and remain in the world, therefore you
> must also share in the blessing which the text
> speaks of in this place.[54]

In discussing the doctrine of the resurrection of the body he
uses an argument *a maiore ad minus:* If we believe that God
created all things out of nothing, we ought to find no difficulty in believing that he is able to raise our bodies. For it is a
lesser thing to make a body out of the dust and ashes to which
it has returned than it is to make the dust out of nothing in
the first place.[55] In the same connection he says that the possibility of a resurrection is a foregone conclusion if we once
grant that God is almighty.[56]

It is evident, then, that Luther did not disparage the processes
of reason as such. A man who could say, "In philosophy a
slight error in the beginning is very great at the end; so in
theology a slight error overthrows the whole body of
doctrine,"[57] certainly did not believe that the processes of
thinking must be left behind when one passes through the
portals of the Christian church.

On the other hand, we must be aware that Luther was not
willing to allow syllogistic argument full and free sway. There
were very definite limitations to be observed in the use of the

logical process. In the debate of January 11, 1539, to which we earlier referred, one of the participants argued that if we take away the reasoning process, we open the door to a completely uncontrolled interpretation of Scripture, and thus with every one free to interpret as he pleases, we will have given men the occasion to become heretics. To this Luther answered,

> Indeed, greater heretics are those who commit the sin of rushing in with the syllogistic form and who permit men to harmonize and to settle everything by reason against Scripture. For, trusting in this form and in reason, they have brought many harmful and vicious conclusions into Scripture, even though a clear text may cry out against it. So we say, "Let the woman ["reason" is a feminine noun in both German and Latin] keep silence in the church." Bring forth something out of Scripture, for it is said, "This is my beloved Son. Listen to him!" Or bring something which will please all your hearers, but only so long as it does not stand and contradict Scripture.[58]

It is clear from these words that Scripture sets the limits beyond which reason is not to go. In this way Luther applied his own axiom, "Theology shall be empress. Philosophy and other good arts shall be her servants. They are not to rule or to govern."[59]

In 1517, before Luther had come to a clear and full understanding of the doctrine of justification by faith, and very likely even before the posting of the ninety-five theses, a disputation was held at Wittenberg on the theology of the scholastics. Luther drew up the theses for this debate. In the forty-seventh of these theses, he wrote, "no syllogistic form holds within the boundaries of the Godhead." But in the very next thesis he laid down the principle, "However, it does not therefore follow that the truth of the doctrine of the Trinity contradicts the syllogistic forms." [60]

And this same position he held toward the close of his life. Twenty-two years later, in a disputation on the sentence, "The Word was made flesh," Luther gave voice to an identical thought in different words. He set up a series of syllogisms, and he held that from a philosophical standpoint they were correct as to form, but that theologically they were wrong. This state of affairs, he said, exists

> not indeed by any fault of the syllogistic form, but because of the excellence of the majesty of the material, which cannot be comprehended in the narrow ways of reason or syllogisms. [61]

If we try, he says, to comprehend the truth of theology in syllogistic forms, we will pour new wine into old bottles and lose them both, as the Sorbonne has done. [62] Evidently, then, Luther was not willing to lose either, and it is to be noted that he guards against giving the impression that he is making an attack upon the syllogism as such. In its place it is a divinely given instrument. But he insists rather that we are here dealing with matters which do not fit into our syllogisms. In regard to the argument,

> Every man is a creature;
> Christ is a man;
> Therefore Christ is a creature,

he says that we really have four terms and therefore no true syllogism. "Man" in the major premise and "man" in the minor premise are not the same thing. In the first it means an ordinary man. In the second it means the incarnate God. [63] This fact, however, is known only to faith, and

> we shall therefore act more correctly, if we
> leave dialectics or philosophy in its own
> sphere and learn to speak with new tongues in
> the realm of faith outside of every sphere.[64]

FAITH AS A RATIONAL PROCESS

Luther would have rejected vehemently and categorically any
point of view which held that men come to faith by rational
conclusion or decision, or that faith is the end product of a
rational process. Of this we shall have more to say in a later
chapter. But this does not in any way mean that reason is not
involved in the believing process. When Luther defined faith
as "right thinking of the heart about God (*rectam cogitationem
cordis de Deo*)," he most certainly looked upon faith as having a
very direct relation to the activities of reason in the human
soul. In the Galatians commentary he wrote, "This right
thinking about God is plainly nothing else than faith."[65]

There are actually places where he defines faith as "right
reason." He often uses the Latin word *ratio,* which is usually
translated as "reason," to denote a way of proceeding, a way of
acting, a way of thinking. Very likely it must be so understood
when he says that when a man becomes a believer, "Another
reason is born which is the reasoning of faith."[66] Yet Luther
did not believe that in conversion any essential change took
place in reason. He specifically says that in substance reason
remains what it was before conversion. If we were then to translate the previous quotation as "another way of thinking is
born, which is faith," this would be in perfect harmony with his
definition of faith as "right thinking of the heart about God."
This would also help us to understand why Luther practically
identifies faith with "right reason," when he says, "In theology
we have no right reason and good will except faith (*in theologia
nullam rectam rationem et bonam voluntatem habemus nisi fidem*)."[67]

Now, for Luther faith was no mere mystical or vague feeling,
as though the "thinking of the heart" were somehow different

from the thinking of the mind. He looked upon faith as an intellectual exercise. In the Galatians commentary he discusses the difference between faith and hope at some length, and he writes, "Faith is in the intellect. Hope is in the will." [68] It is in this same connection that he says, "First of all, a pious man ought to have a right opinion and intellect informed by faith." "Informed by faith" means that faith governs the intellect. Just a few lines later he writes, "Faith therefore is the dialectic which conceives an idea of all that is believed." [69]

Luther regularly treats faith as the receiving instrument by which the individual believer appropriates the merits of Christ. In the commentary on Galatians there is a paragraph in which he speaks of the "apprehension of Christ through faith." But of surpassing significance for our thesis is the previous sentence, which reads, "However, Christ is apprehended not by the law, not by works, but by reason, or the intellect, illumined by faith." [70]

This conception of a reason which is "informed" or "illumined" by faith is commonplace in Luther. He was willing to listen to reason wherever it was "grounded" in Scripture. [71] In the commentary on Genesis, he describes what happens to a man in conversion.

> Faith is a change and renewal of the whole nature, so that ears, eyes, and the heart itself hear, see, and feel something entirely new. . . . For faith is living and powerful. It is not idle thinking. It does not swim on top of the heart, as a goose on water, but just as water, warmed by fire, although it remains water, nevertheless is no longer cold, but warm and entirely different water, so faith, the work of the Holy Spirit, constructs another mind and feeling, and makes an entirely new man. [72]

As we have already seen, Luther held that our judgment, our reason and our intellect are defiled and corrupted through original sin.[73] Because of that the "light" of reason is turned into darkness. And because reason is darkened, all the powers of man are used improperly, for "where reason leads, the will follows."[74] These words of Luther express a thought which is almost identical with that to which Jonathan Edwards gives voice when he says, "The will always follows the last dictate of the understanding."[75]

But in conversion reason is renewed. Luther compares the procedure by which a man comes to faith to that by which a snake sheds its skin, and he says of man,

> So he sheds the old skin, leaves behind his light, his thinking, his willing, his loving, his desiring, his speaking, his acting; and so he becomes an entirely new man, who sees all things differently from before, judges different-ly, decides differently, thinks differently, wills differently, speaks differently, loves differently, desires differently, acts and conducts himself differently from the way that he had done.[76]

Thus the reason of man is purified[77] and enlightened by faith.[78] When someone asked Luther whether the light of reason were of any use or advantage to a theologian, he answered that we must distinguish between reason possessed by the devil and reason illumined by the Spirit. He said that it is with reason as with all the members of the body. The tongue of the unbeliever utters blasphemies, but the tongue of a believer is used to praise God. Insofar as its substance is concerned, it is a tongue before conversion and after conver-sion. There is no change in its essence.

> And the tongue, so far as it is a tongue, does not help faith, and still it serves faith, when

the heart is purified (or, enlightened, *illustratum est*). So also reason, when it is purified *(illustrata)*, serves faith in thinking about a thing. But without faith reason profits nothing and can do nothing, just as the tongue without faith speaks nothing but blasphemies, as we see in Duke George. But reason purified takes all its thoughts from the Word. The substance remains, but the vanity departs when reason is purified *(illustratur)* by the Spirit.[79]

The grace of God in conversion does not change the nature of man, however, insofar as its temperament or its gifts and talents are concerned. It uses nature as it finds it. If a man is mild-mannered before conversion, he becomes a mild-mannered Christian. If he has a fiery nature, he becomes a fiery preacher. And where grace finds a sharp, versatile man, gifted with reason, as Philip Melanchthon, there it uses such a man for the salvation of others.[80]

Reason indeed does not help a man come to faith, but once the power of the Holy Ghost has kindled faith in the heart, faith uses reason as an excellent servant.

Reason acts and serves in matters of faith not before but after conversion, just as the tongue and all human powers and members of the body. Reason, after it is enlightened by the Holy Spirit, serves faith. But without faith it blasphemes God together with all powers and members of the body, both outward and inward.[81]

Thus in the believer reason becomes what Luther calls the "best instrument of piety."[82] He continues,

Reason receives life from faith. It is put to death by it and made alive again. Just as our body will rise in a glorified state, so also our

reason is different after conversion from what
it was before. The same thing must be said
about our memory, our will, and our tongue.
All things are changed, just as glowing iron is
changed into something different from that
which is not glowing. This is the regeneration
through the Word, which, although the members and the person remain the same, yet
changes the members and makes another person from that which was conceived and born
from Adam.[83]

It is clear from all this that the antirationalism of Luther is
never "irrationalism," as Bainton wrongly describes it. When
God works in an eloquent man, God makes use of his
eloquence. When he works in an energetic man, he works in
and through his energy. When he works in a rational man, he
operates through and with his rationality. Although a man
contributes absolutely nothing to his conversion to the
Christian faith nor to his preservation in that faith, and all
things in this realm are done by God, yet God works in us in
such a way that we work with him.

Man is a rational creature,[84] and he remains a rational creature
also after his conversion to the Christian faith. His rationality
acquires a new attitude and a new direction indeed, but essentially it is no different from what it has always been. The rules
of logic are the same for the believer as for the unbeliever,
wherever they apply. But by acquiring this new outlook reason
becomes an excellent instrument for apprehending the truth of
Scripture, for understanding its words, for determining its
meaning, for communicating the message to others. "A fluent
tongue promotes faith," says Luther. "Reason makes the
sermon clear, and all things help faith."[85] But, said Luther at
the Heidelberg debate in May of 1518, just as the sex urge is
not used properly unless a person is married, so "no one
philosophizes well except a fool, that is, a Christian."[86]

CHAPTER IV

REASON AS JUDGE OF BIBLICAL TRUTH

We have seen how Luther exalted and praised reason as a great gift of God when it comes to understanding what the Bible wants to say to us in its human but divinely chosen and inspired words. In spite of all the nasty things he has to say about reason, Luther nevertheless leaves some room for reason as a source of innate religious knowledge, as a useful tool in combatting error if not for establishing the truth, and especially as an instrument for the apprehending of the truths revealed by God for our salvation.

In this chapter we shall deal with Luther's estimate of reason as judge of religious truth, or better, Biblical truth. It is here that we will find Luther's most intense fulminations against reason. It is in this area that he has absolutely nothing good to say about reason. It is here that we will find especially those remarks which are so common in Luther and which have led John Wesley and many others to see the great reformer as a thoroughgoing irrationalist. We must admit that Luther, by his vehement condemnations of reason, does give apparent cause for this interpretation and for the claim that he is the father, or at least one of the fathers, of what has been called the modern religious revolt against reason. Disparagements of reason are scattered throughout his works. And if these disparagements are read apart from the wider context of Luther's total point of view, they can lead to no other picture of the reformer's attitude toward reason.

Before rendering a final judgment, however, we dare not forget the evidence submitted in the previous chapters, which clearly demonstrates that Luther cannot rightly be classified as an irrationalist. There was a place, and an important place, for reason in his theology. Luther did value reason highly as the instrument by which a person intellectually understands and apprehends the Word of God. Yet we have also heard him say that it is one thing to understand the Word of God and quite another thing to believe it and to accept it. And one of the greatest obstacles to the acceptance of the truth of the Word of God is this same reason by which it is apprehended mentally and understood. Luther was convinced that the better a person understands the Word of God the harder it is for him to believe it.

Of all the aspects of Luther's thought on the subject of reason, this is the most difficult to assess and to evaluate. This is the case, first of all, because of the tremendous amount of material that we can summon on the subject. You can open Luther almost anywhere and without much searching find some disparaging remark about reason. To sift and to analyze this mass of material is in itself a baffling task.

Secondly, when Luther denounces reason, he often seems to mean much more by that term than it usually denotes. Some scholars have suggested that when Luther speaks in the context of faith, he does not mean reason at all when he speaks of *Vernunft*. Bainton, for example, believes that it would be better to translate *"Vernunft"* as "common sense." He writes,

> At Worms and often elsewhere he asked to be instructed from Scripture and reason. In this sense reason meant logical deduction from known premises; but when Luther railed against the harlot reason he meant something else. Common sense is perhaps a better translation. He had in mind the way in which man ordinarily behaves, feels, and thinks.[1]

While there is much in Bainton's view which is acceptable, it will be clear after a thorough examination of what Luther actually says on this matter that such a solution is not entirely adequate.

LUTHER'S REJECTION OF EMPIRICAL THEOLOGY

While Luther does not say so, yet it often seems that in his raging against reason he was directly attacking the dictum of St. Thomas that nothing is in the intellect that is not previously in the senses. We have already dealt with Luther's recognition of an *a priori* knowledge (the natural knowledge) of God, and we should remember this when we begin to consider Luther's attack on reason as judge. On the other hand, we should also remember that Luther recognized that the Word of God comes to men through the medium of human speech, that is, in the normal way that human speech is understood, by the exercise of the reasoning powers of human nature.

But while the form of the Word, that is, the language and the grammar in which it is couched, is subject to the judgment of reason and sense, the content of the Word is beyond all sense and reason. As far as sense and reason are concerned, both believers and unbelievers see the same thing in the Word. They hear the same words. They see the same events. Thus, for example, the Jews looked at Jesus of Nazareth and they saw him shamefully crucified, killed and buried. And they judged him by what they saw. They considered Jesus of Nazareth to be pure error and deception, nothing but lies and dreams, pure death and hellish poison. The Christian sees the same thing as the Jew, and for him, too, Jesus is shamefully crucified, and killed, and buried, but the Lord says to his disciples,

> If you want to know me in the right way, you must not follow your eyes and carnal understanding, as the Jews do, but you must grasp the Word that you hear from me in your heart, hold fast to it, and judge only

> according to it. Thus you will learn how I
> pass through weakness, cross, death and all
> things, and come to the Father.[2]

It is the very nature of reason, says Luther, to judge only by
what it sees. In this it is diametrically opposed to faith, for
faith judges by what it does not see, "while reason is accustomed to lean on present things, faith embraces those that are
absent, and, contrary to reason, it judges them to be present."[3]
Human reason cannot go beyond judging by what it sees with
its eyes, or feels, or grasps by the senses. Faith, however, judges
independently of and even against the data furnished by the
senses and clings only to that which is offered in the Word.
Luther sounds this note repeatedly.[4] He says that reason
judges only according to that which it sees. What it does not
see it cannot understand.[5]

When Abraham was called by God to leave all that was dear
to him and to go to an unknown place, this was a severe trial
to his flesh. It is significant, incidentally, that Luther says
"flesh" in this connection, for in the whole context he speaks
about the unwillingness of "reason" to accept the Word of
God. The flesh recoils from such a command as that given to
Abraham and considers it a shame to leave what is present and
to chase after absent things. He goes on to say,

> The true promises of God consistently
> hold out the cross, but after the cross they
> promise a blessing. Reason, on both counts, is
> offended. The things it does not see and
> which are far away it considers to be nothing.
> But from the cross it turns away and flees it
> as though it were an eternal evil that will
> never come to an end.[6]

Reason is able to arrange in order the things which are subject
to our five senses. But here are its limits. Reason can do

nothing more than to look at visible phenomena.[7] "Reason," Luther says, "judges according to isolated instances and beginnings of evils, not according to the Word and the promising God."[8] Faith, however, proceeds in an entirely different way. It clings only to the Word of God and guides itself by those things which it does not see, but which it knows only from the Word.[9] The real nature of faith is that it

> follows nothing but the bare Word, even if it is contrary to all sense and contends against all human reason, yes, against its own senses and everything that it sees, feels, and hears.[10]

When Noah was called upon to build the ark, he had to endure the scorn and the mockery of his fellowmen. There must have been times when his own reason rebelled and when he found it difficult to obey the command of the Lord. But he simply closed his eyes and smothered his reason and held fast to the Word.[11] From this story of Noah, Luther then draws the conclusion:

> So faith must tread underfoot all reason, sense, and understanding. It puts everything that it sees out of sight and wants to know nothing but God's Word.[12]

By faith we see just the opposite of what we experience with our senses. In death the Christian sees life. In God's wrath and judgment we see righteousness. In the bad conscience we see peace and salvation. In God's anger we see his goodness and mercy.[13] Thus God lets the wicked prosper—just to give us an opportunity to exercise our faith and to learn that we are to judge not by what we see but by what we do not see.[14] So also God lets all his works stand in contradiction to reason, so that reason judges that nothing can come of them and that his words and promises are nothing at all. But God acts as he does because he wants to put proud reason to shame and to accustom his saints to trust in him alone.[15] This is an important and very practical lesson, for when evil days come to the child of God, he must learn that God always hides his "Yes" under a "No."[16]

> All this is done that we may learn to look at our troubles not according to reason but with Christian eyes. Those are eyes which, when they look at death, sin, and hell, say, "I see no death; I feel no sin; I am not damned; but through Christ I see nothing but holiness, life, and salvation." Likewise, when I am poor, I feel no poverty and it seems to me that I have enough, for I have Christ who can at all times give me what I need, even if I have nothing.[17]

It is clear that when Luther in all these passages speaks against reason, he has in mind what we might call empirical theology. Luther did not want men to believe that God answers prayer because they could point to a thousand instances in which it was manifest that prayers had been answered. He knew that it was possible to find just as many instances in which it appeared that prayers had not been answered. He said that we must learn to put out of our sight whatever the flesh is able to comprehend, and, believing the Word, "hold just the opposite of what we know and feel and see."[18] This is what he meant when he said that faith is "against philosophy and human reason."[19] Faith, he said, would continue to believe that God is good even if he were to damn all men.[20]

And just as reason is inclined to judge by what it sees, so it is guided also by what it feels. If it does not feel, it immediately denies God and says, "God is not here."[21] For example, philosophy and reason can think of sin only as a quality which inheres in a subject just as color inheres in a wall, and it cannot believe that sin is removed until it is replaced by the opposite quality. But according to the Word of God, the sins of the world are no longer where they are seen and felt. According to philosophy and reason sin and death are nowhere else but in the world, but the Word tells us that there is no more sin in the world because it has been taken away by the Lamb of God.[22]

Because of this basic conflict between faith and reason—that is, between the conclusions drawn on the basis of the words and the promises of God and the conclusions based on the data of experience—we must "against all reason and sense" cling to the Word alone.[23] Luther was always insistent on this, that we should never under any circumstances base our faith on our experience. If experience happens to bear out the conclusions of faith, as may sometimes be the case, this is all to the good; but we must never in any way look upon experience as validating the conclusions of faith. In nature, in the realm of sense and reason, experience always precedes assent. But this is never the case in true theology. There experience invariably follows assent.[24]

Manifestly, therefore, one thing Luther wanted to say with many of his attacks on reason was this, that we are not to let any empirical evidence or sensory experience influence or determine our attitude over against the Word of God. To Luther the Word was to be sole basis of faith. Moreover, it is the Word of *God*. As such it remains true and firm in spite of all appearances to the contrary. In fact, it is *necessary* that appearances should be against God's Word. Only under those conditions is there room for faith, and only in such a situation can we learn to trust in the Word alone. Faith is firm conviction about unseen things. Here again the Lutheran watchword of *sola Scriptura* becomes operative. Scripture is not only the sole source of all Christian doctrine, but also the sole basis of faith. Luther writes,

> Reason follows only what it can see. But it must be put to death, so that the Word and faith may have a place. However, reason cannot be put to death, except through despair,

> mistrust, hatred, and murmuring against God,
> so that at length, when all external objects
> have been removed, the soul may cling to and
> rest in only the Word and the sacraments.[25]

To Luther this was always a very practical matter, one with deep significance for the daily life of the Christian. The kingdom of Christ is a kingdom of the cross. Christians are people who must endure persecution and suffer more than other men.[26] They often feel that God has forsaken them and they see their suffering as a punishment which reminds them of their sins. But when our sins press upon us most heavily, he says,

> we must press the Word alone upon our heart
> and weave ourselves into it and learn this
> skill, which makes it possible for us to accuse
> our own heart of lying and to set the Word
> over against it. For it alone must remain true,
> and everything that speaks against it must be
> a lying invention and an untruth.[27]

We must hold fast to the Word, always keep it firmly in mind, and with it fight against all questioning, all philosophizing, and all disputing.[28] Thus we must believe that we are lords over the devil even while we feel that we are defeated by him.[29] We must learn to believe, prior to all experience, what man simply cannot believe and to feel what we do not feel.[30] Any other course must inevitably lead to disaster.

> If you do not want to let the Word count for
> more than all your feelings, eyes, senses, and
> heart, you must be lost; there is no help for
> you. For this is called an article of faith, not
> of your reason nor of wisdom nor of the
> power and ability of men. Therefore, here you
> must judge only according to the Word and
> pay no attention to what you feel or see.[31]

In this way the children of God learn to know that God is nearest just at the moment when he seems to be farthest away. At the time when he seems to be most angry, when he sends them afflictions and trials, they know him best as their merciful Savior. When they feel the terrors of sin and death most deeply, then they know best that they have eternal right-eousness. And just when they are of all men the most miser-able they know that they are lords over all things.[32]

This is a theme which recurs in Luther's theology again and again, and to those who have not seen in their own lives how basic this approach is to the assurance of the Christian, it must seem like monotonous repetition. But we can sense how much it meant to Luther himself when we hear him say that the Word of God is above and against all reason and then continue,

> "I forgive you!" There, you hear the word. You see sin, but even though you are absolved, you do not feel that God and his angels are smil-ing at you. Of that friendship you know nothing at all. You have, after all, the same hand after baptism and absolution that you had before. Therefore it is nothing. Nothing? No, no! You should say, "God has baptized and absolved me, and now I believe that God smiles at me and that the angels rejoice over me. I do not see these things, but I should believe them. The angels smile at me; God calls me his son; Christ calls me his brother." That you must not doubt. Even if the pope does not believe this, that does you no harm.[33]

THE TENDENCY OF REASON TO JUDGE ON THE BASIS OF INADEQUATE EVIDENCE

Faith humbles itself before God and clings to his Word as the source of wisdom and truth. Reason, on the other hand, in its corruption and pride, always makes the mistake of exalting its very limited experience and equating it with omniscience. When Luther says that reason judges by the "isolated instances and beginnings" of evil, he points to a basic weakness of the Aristotelian and scholastic approach to truth. It is the very nature of inductive reasoning that most of its universals are theoretical constructions. Reason is not able to acquire universal truth just because man is not God. The experience of man is always limited to isolated moments (*puncta et principia*) in the vast expanse of time and space. Even at their highest reaches the senses can acquire knowledge that is merely fragmentary. Self-evident as this is, men in practice tend to forget it.

In itself the fragmentary character of all empirical knowledge would not be to reason's dishonor. If man were satisfied to be a creature of God, limited and circumscribed by his own nature, on the one hand, and by the will of God, on the other, reason would remain an excellent instrument. But again we must call attention to the corruption and depravity of fallen reason. Instead of viewing the data of experience as precious gifts of God, who has given us all things richly to enjoy, men exalt their limited experience to the point where they consider themselves competent to sit in judgment over God. And so, Luther says, they become as godless as Erasmus, who thinks that God is unjust when he does ill to the good and well to the wicked.[34]

> Such an Epicurean and ungodly opinion
> about God comes from this, that they feel
> that our natural powers are whole. They do
> not see that our judgment and our reason and
> intellect have been vitiated and corrupted
> through original sin. Therefore they think
> that God is such as they perceive him to be
> through their sick eyes. They are wearing blue
> glasses, and through them they also look at
> God and imagine that he is as they see him.
> And they cannot see him differently. For they
> do not see the magnitude of the evil which

original sin has brought about for us and how
corrupt our judgment has become.[35]

Thus reason in its sinful pride and presumption always tends
to make wholes out of parts and to raise particulars to the
level of universals. When it sees something happen a few
times, it immediately assumes that it always happens the same
way. Having done this, it proceeds to permit its fabricated
universals to sit in judgment on God and his Word.[36] It was
this error of reason that Luther often had in mind when he
attacked reason. Therefore he would have viewed the extrapo-
lations of modern science with righteous scorn.

And Luther would very likely have been amazed and annoyed
to hear anyone accuse him of irrationalism on this account.
He himself believed that reason was foolish and unreasonable
in its presumption, for in the Genesis commentary he wrote,

> What, however, is more absurd than that we
> should assume the right to judge God and his
> Word, since we should have been judged by
> God? Therefore in this matter we must sim-
> ply insist that when we hear God say anything
> we will believe it and not argue, but rather
> take our intellect captive in obedience to
> Christ.[37]

It is, of course, true that if we judge according to the fragmentary knowledge and the limited experience of reason, the
things which God makes known to us in his Word seem
impossible and absurd. And when the enemies of the Word
point this out to us, they tell us only what we already know
and understand as well as they.[38] For what does God tell us in
the Scriptures?

> Impossible things, lies, foolish things, weak
> things, absurdities, abomination, heresies and

> diabolical things!—if you ask reason for
> advice. . . . It is always the case that when God
> sets articles of faith before us, he conveys to
> us things that are simply impossible and
> absurd—if you wish to follow the judgment
> of reason.[39]

The words and promises of God seem impossible and absurd
to reason on at least three counts. First, they often seem to be
entirely out of harmony with our present fragmentary experience. When we see the Christians overwhelmed by sorrow and
suffering and by the enmity of the entire world, it

> just does not seem fit that such poor, miser-
> able beings . . . should possess the great things
> of which the Scriptures tell us—that we
> should be eternal heirs of God in heaven, live,
> and be saved alone through faith and bap-
> tism, even though we are now indeed still
> subject to sin and death.[40]

Reason looks only at the present troubles. Because it knows
nothing about the promises of God regarding the future, it is
easily overwhelmed by them. But "the Holy Spirit commands
us to disregard the present and to look to the future."[41] And
the knowledge of the future is open only to faith. It can be
known in no other way. Commenting on the words of Psalm
23:1, "I shall not want," Luther says that it seems to reason
that the very reverse of these words is true. It seems

> that on earth there are no poorer, more miser-
> able, and unhappier people than those very
> Christians. . . . It appears outwardly that the
> Christians are scattered sheep, forsaken by
> God, already handed over to the jaws of the
> wolves—sheep who lack nothing except
> everything (den nichts denn nur alles mangele). . . .

Therefore, I say, do not in this matter follow
the world and your reason. People become
fools over this and consider the prophet to be
a liar when he says, "I shall not want," because
they judge according to outward appearance.
But, as we said previously, stick to God's Word
and promise, listen to your shepherd, how and
what he speaks to you, and follow his voice,
not what your eyes see and your heart feels. In
this way you have conquered.[42]

In the second place, reason finds the Word of God to be
absurd because the ways of God are sometimes completely out
of harmony with man's customary way of thinking. Erasmus,
in his defense of the free will of man, argued that it is absurd
to say that God, who is both just and good, should harden a
man. Luther admits readily that reason is offended by this
doctrine.[43] But in reply to this argument of Erasmus, he says,

So now absurdity is one of the principal reasons why we do not simply accept the words
of Moses and Paul! . . . With that same argument you will deny all the articles of faith. . . .
For if reason is the judge, it remains absurd
that the just and good God demands from
the free will what it cannot render—when the
free will cannot desire what is good and can
only serve sin, God nevertheless holds it
responsible. . . . Reason will say that a good
and merciful God does not do such things.[44]

In the third place, reason considers the truth of God to be
absurd and impossible because it often seems to violate the
laws of logic. Logic argues, for example, that the doctrine of
the Trinity does not square with its rules.[45] In the incarnation
of the Son of God there is a joining together of the finite and
the infinite, which is manifestly impossible.[46] And when men

tell us that one is not three and that three is not one, and that man is not God and that the Creator is not a creature, that the potter is not the pot, and that the shoes are not the cobbler,[47] we gladly admit that such things are true

> when we speak of potters and cobblers and those things of which reason can and should judge. But here it is not right that we should attempt to apply a skill of which our heads are not capable. Here we are dealing with God's Word, revealed from heaven. Here you must simply take off your little hat and say yes to it and let it be true, as something that did not emerge from your understanding. Here you must simply not want to know or to understand, but you must consider yourself to be a fool with that great cerebral skill of yours which tells you that three is not one and that the pots are not the potter. Here we are in a different university, where the subject is not what I and other men understand but what God himself says and teaches.[48]

Thus reason is the greatest hindrance to faith, because it deems the things of God to be absurd nonsense.[49]

It is possible to cite countless examples of how Luther applies these principles in discussing the doctrines of the Christian faith. He freely and repeatedly admits that the Lutheran doctrines of the Lord's Supper and baptism are not in harmony with the conclusions of reason. He writes,

> Reason . . . can only say, "Bread is bread, and water is water. How can bread be Christ's body or water be a bath for souls?" Reason cannot and will not stay in the Word and surrender to it. . . . Reason sees that the Word

> defies all understanding, that it is against
> every sense, feeling and experience. So reason
> falls away from the Word of God or denies it
> completely or, if it cannot avoid it, turns and
> twists that Word with comments until it
> finally agrees with reason. But then faith has
> no more place. Faith has to give way and con-
> cede the victory to reason.[50]

There is absolutely no evidence for the real presence of the
body and blood of Christ in the Lord's Supper except in the
Words of Christ, "This is my body. . . . This is my blood."
And these words ought to be believed. "They ought not and
they cannot be understood."[51] Of his doctrine Luther said,

> There I will not first ask reason about it, but
> I will hear what the Lord Christ says about it
> and close my eyes. . . . I will only hear what
> the Lord says, namely, that I should eat his
> flesh and drink his blood. More I do not
> have. By this I will stay. I have heard these
> words. I will believe them and stick with
> them. I do not see it. I cannot figure it out.
> Let it fit itself into my head as it may. In this
> way I will listen to these words.[52]

In this same matter Luther resolved never to be guided by the
experience of his senses.

> I indeed hear the words, but what they say I
> do not feel, touch or see. But still I will stick
> with them and cling to them and die in this
> conviction (undt dorauff sterben).[53]

Luther did not hesitate to admit that his doctrine of the
Lord's Supper was difficult to believe. He put the objections
of the sacramentarians into these words,

How can a body sit so exalted in glory and at
the same time be down here and permit itself
to be disgraced and handled with the hands,
the mouth and the stomach, as though it were
a sausage? How does that agree with the glorious majesty and the heavenly glory?[54]

In a sermon which he preached to this congregation in 1530
he spoke of this same doctrine in much the same way and said
that when reason comes to this teaching it thinks:

"I must bite him to pieces like a piece of
beef or as the dogs tear a piece of meat with
their teeth and eat it up and chew it for
themselves. How can this one man be eaten
by the whole world? For if he were as large as
the largest hills or as the Alps, he would still
not be enough." Reason speculates much
about it. And because it cannot understand it
(dieweil es nicht reichen kann), it concludes that it
cannot be right.[55]

Luther grants freely that the doctrine of the real presence does
not agree with reason. But he says that if we are to judge the
doctrine of our faith and the Scriptures according to reason
and sight (der vernunfft und augen nach), we will find that every
part of Scripture is against every other part.[56] To all the objections of the sacramentarians, he replies sarcastically,

My thanks to you, kind sirs, I did not know
that in articles of faith one must ask nothing
about God's word but open the bodily eyes
and with them judge, according to reason,
what is to be believed. Now I understand
what that means, that faith has to do with
unseen things. According to the new interpretation of these spirits it means that faith

should believe no more than that which the
eyes can point to with the fingers and which
reason can comprehend.[57]

In Luther's theology the doctrine of the Lord's Supper was
closely allied to the doctrine of the person of Christ. In the
doctrine of the real presence, the doctrine of the complete
and total unity of the personality of the God-man was at
stake.[58] If the first is rejected on the ground that it is an
absurdity in the opinion of reason, then the second must be
rejected also, for, as Luther says,

> God is man, the son of a virgin, crucified, sit-
> ting at the right hand of the Father. It is
> absurd, I say, to believe such things. Let us
> make up some figure of speech with the
> Manichaeans, so that he may not be a true
> man, but a phantom passing through the vir-
> gin as a ray of light through glass and cruci-
> fied. So beautifully we will handle Scripture![59]

Reason, says Luther, simply cannot comprehend or believe that
he who measures the heavens with a span should lie in a narrow
manger and suckle at his mother's breast.[60] Unlike Zwingli and
the Roman theologians, he resisted every tendency to separate
the two natures within the one person so sharply that the acts
of the God-man were distributed.[61] He knew, indeed, that
reason would have its problems with the personal union in
Christ and that it would "make it agree slowly."[62] But this is not
a sound basis for rejecting divine truth.

In 1545 Luther presided at a disputation in Wittenberg at
which one of the theses under discussion read,

> This person, at one and the same time finite
> and infinite, is made the servant of sinners
> and the newest and weakest of all things. This

is unbelievable, but to those who believe it, it
is most joyful.[63]

The same doctrine had been discussed at the university in
1539, when a disputation was held on the question whether
the statement, "The Word was made flesh," could be defended
on philosophical and logical grounds. Luther held that while
this statement is most certainly true in theology, yet "in
philosophy it is simply impossible and absurd."[64] The third
thesis drawn up for this disputation reads, "It is not less, but
more, disparate to preach, 'God is man,' than to say, 'A man is
a donkey.' If this doctrine is to be believed, reason must be
killed completely, for according to the judgment of reason
such a doctrine is manifestly impossible."[65]

The same thing must be said about the doctrine of the Trinity.
Here reason can do no more than say,

> It is impossible and a contradiction that there
> are three Persons, each one the complete
> God, and yet that there is no more than one
> single God, and that only the Son is man, and
> that whoever has the Father and the Son will
> also, from the Father and the Son, know the
> Holy Spirit well.[66]

But these apparent absurdities and impossibilities are not
limited to the Godhead, where we might expect to find them.
The doctrine of the resurrection of the body presents the very
game kind of difficulty for the reason of men. When men seek
to think through this article with their reason, "They imagine
such wondrous, strange, and irreconcilable thoughts, that they
must say that there is nothing to it (es sey nichts dran)."[67]

Abraham was faced with the same sort of absurdity and
impossibility when God promised him that Sarah would give
birth to a son. Luther asks,

> What is more ridiculous, foolish and impos-
> sible than when God said to Abraham that he
> was about to receive a son out of the barren
> and dead flesh of Sarah?[68]

Abraham's reason did not accept his promise easily. Reason
fought in him against faith and held it to be ridiculous, absurd,
and impossible that Sarah, who was not only ninety years old
but also barren by nature, should bear a son.

> Faith certainly had this struggle with reason
> in Abraham. But faith conquered in him,
> butchered and sacrificed that bitterest and
> most pestilential enemy of God. Likewise all
> the pious, stepping with Abraham into the
> darkness *(tenebras)* of faith, put reason to
> death and say, "Reason, you are a fool. You
> do not know the things of God. So do not
> get in my way, but be quiet. Do not judge, but
> hear the Word of God and believe."[69]

It is surely of some significance that Luther here tells reason
to be quiet, to get out of the way, to refrain from judging. Yet,
he is still addressing that same reason when he says, "Hear the
Word and believe."

In the light of these words of Luther, then, we can understand why he sometimes simply equates "unbelief" with
"natural reason."[70] To the unbeliever the gospel is always a
"foolish doctrine."[71]

> It certainly seems ridiculous and absurd to
> reason that in the Supper there is offered to
> us the body and blood of Christ, that bap-
> tism is a washing of regeneration and renew-
> ing of the Holy Ghost, that the dead will rise
> at the last day, that Christ, the Son of God,

was conceived and carried in the womb of the
virgin, that he was born, and that he suffered
a most shameful death on the cross.[72]

Because of this conflict between reason and faith, Luther
often speaks of the necessity of putting reason to death.
According to the *Tischreden*,[73] he said that reason is killed by all
the articles of the Christian faith.[74] In his comments on the
story of Abraham and Sarah, he said of reason,

> Faith butchered and killed this beast which all
> the world and all creatures cannot kill.
> Abraham killed it with faith in the word of
> God by which a seed was promised to him
> out of barren and worn-out Sarah.[75]

When the godly slay this beast they are bringing the sacrifice
which is most pleasing to God. In comparison to it, all the
works of the monks are nothing.

> For in making this sacrifice the godly first
> kill reason, the greatest and most invincible
> enemy of God, which despises God and
> denies his wisdom, justice, virtue, truth,
> mercy, majesty, and divinity. Then through
> this same sacrifice they give glory to God,
> that is, they believe him to be just, good,
> faithful, true, etc. They believe that he can
> do all things, that all his words are holy,
> true, living, powerful, etc. This is the wor-
> ship most pleasing to God. Therefore there
> is no greater, better, or more pleasing reli-
> gion or worship to be found in the world
> than faith.[76]

This, he says, is the daily morning and evening sacrifice which
the children of God bring in the New Testament. The

morning sacrifice is to put reason to death, and the evening sacrifice is to bring glory to God.[77]

At times Luther becomes very vehement on this subject. If we were to follow reason, he said in one of his sermons, we would all become Mohammedans.[78] This was a bitter pill to administer to a world in which scholastic theology had kindled the hope of winning the Mohammedans for Christianity by an appeal to reason. In the same sermon Luther continues, with sharp ridicule,

> According to reason, we want to be masters over our Lord God and teach him what fits and does not fit. And if it does not fit, then friend, throw the doctrine out! So, for example, it makes no sense to sprinkle children with the water of baptism. Throw the doctrine out! In this way we will construct a right faith. . . . According to reason we are as intelligent in these matters as a cow. And if intelligence counted for anything, I could probably construct a religion better than you. But here, we are not in a tavern. We are in a Christian church, where we must believe, not what reason thinks is right or what pleases me or you, but what the Scriptures tell us.[79]

Against all the objections of reason we are to stick to God's Word, no matter how it sounds (es klappe, laute, oder klinge wie es wolle).[80]

We might almost say that Luther died with a warning against reason on his lips. He spoke of it in the last sermon that he preached to his congregation in Wittenberg. In it he described reason as that mangy, leprous whore, the foremost whore the devil has. And he spoke of it again in the very last sermon of

his life, a sermon delivered at Eisenach just three days before
he died. He told his hearers there that they should pray,

> Dear heavenly Father, speak. I will gladly be a
> fool and a child and be still. For if I were to
> govern with my intelligence, wisdom, and rea-
> son, the cart would have been stuck in the
> mud long ago, and the ship would have been
> shattered. Therefore, dear God, govern and
> rule it yourself. I will gladly stab out my eyes
> and shut up reason and let the rule belong to
> you alone through the Word.[81]

LUTHER'S ATTACK ON THE LEGALISM OF REASON

Luther had yet another ground for his enmity against reason.
To him the very essence of Christianity was the doctrine of
salvation by grace alone. He considered the doctrine of justification by faith to be the very heart of the Christian religion.
But, as we have already seen, Luther believed that all men are
born with a legalistic concept of salvation. We have seen also
that he held that it was the habit of human reason to look at
all things through its "blue glasses"—which means nothing
more than that man's natural way of thinking about salvation
will always judge God's way of salvation to be untrue and will
resist it to the death.

> This beast, which is called reason, is the
> chief fountain of evils. Because it does not
> fear, it does not love God, it does not trust
> God, but thoughtlessly it despises him. It
> is moved neither by his threats nor his
> promises; it does not delight in his words
> and works, but murmurs against God; it is
> angry with him; it judges and hates God; in
> short, reason is an enemy of God (Romans 8).
> It does not give him the glory. If this beast,

that is, reason, were killed, these external
and gross sins would be nothing.[82]

Viewed in this context, reason certainly includes far more
than we commonly understand under that term. Reason is
the basic, innate set of attitudes with which a man comes
into the world. Those who have taken their philosophical
presuppositions from John Locke and Immanuel Kant,
however, will have difficulty in understanding Luther's fulminations against reason.

Even the Lutheran confessions speak of a righteousness of
reason, or philosophical righteousness. But while natural man
knows this kind of righteousness, reason is completely ignorant of the righteousness of faith, which is ours for Christ's
sake.[83] Unless God acts in full accord with the principles laid
down in the code of Justinian or in the fifth book of
Aristotle's *Ethics,* men simply will not believe that he is good
and just.[84] Man is born with a sense of justice, which means
nothing more nor less than that he knows, without being
taught, that the good ought to be rewarded and that the evil
ought to be punished. Therefore, according to human reason,
God must reward the good and punish the sinner. If we want
to follow reason, it is just as unfair to crown those who are
unworthy of coronation as it is to punish those who are
unworthy of punishment.[85] On this account, human beings, if
they are guided by reason, must fall either into despair or into
self-righteousness. Either they will believe that they are good
and that God will reward them on that account, in which case
they do not know themselves as sinners; or they believe that
they are evil and that therefore God will punish them, in which
case they do not know the forgiving love of Christ. In either
case they do not believe what the Scriptures tell them about
themselves and about God.[86] It is on this ground that Luther
practically equates reason with unbelief.[87] It is especially in the
doctrine of justification that reason is the enemy of faith.[88]

So when the conscience has been frightened by the law, we must not ask counsel of reason. For once the law and reason have joined forces, the virginity of faith has been violated. These two, the law and reason, can be subdued only with great effort, but subdued they must be if we are to be saved at all. When our conscience troubles us, we must act as if we had never heard of the law, Luther says.

> Go up into the darkness, where neither law nor reason shines, where only the riddle of faith (*aenigma fidei*) resides—faith which firmly holds that salvation is outside of and beyond the law, in Christ. Thus the gospel leads us beyond and above the light of the law and of reason into the darkness of faith (*tenebras fidei*), where law and reason have no business. The law must be heard, but in its own place and time.[89]

In his Word God gives us a far different picture of himself than that which is native to our reason. He tells us that if we want to please him, we are not to offer him our works.[90] But men find it very difficult to give up the belief that the way to divine favor is through human merit.[91] This is the way of salvation which the monks have chosen under the guidance of their reason.[92] This is what the pope also teaches. And human reason is pleased with his doctrine and delights in this lie. It gladly hears that it can by its own works merit salvation. With this doctrine the pope does not put reason to death but he makes it alive. The flesh (note that here again Luther equates flesh with reason) easily accepts this teaching and believes these promises without question or debate.[93]

But God tells us, contrary to all human reason, that he is pleased with us for the sake of his Son, who was born, suffered, was crucified and died for us. In him we should put our trust. Through him we are in God's favor, and by his work our sins are taken away. When reason hears this, it says, "Are my good works then worth nothing at all; have I borne the burden and the heat of the day for nothing?"[94] This is what Luther means when he says that through faith we kill reason.[95] In fact, either reason or faith must die in this battle.

> Unless therefore reason is butchered and all religions and worship under heaven excogitated by men for winning righteousness before God are damned, the righteousness of faith cannot stand.[96]

But even believers must constantly struggle against this beast. For on account of their reason and human nature they do not hold Christ firmly in their arms.[97] Reason simply does not have the innate capacity to think rightly about God. This can be done only by faith.[98] In the Galatians commentary he says,

> By reason I am not able to apprehend or to hold with certainty that I am received into grace on account of Christ, but I hear this announced through the gospel and apprehend it by faith.[99]

Unless we are willing to say that Luther was hopelessly confused in his thinking and that he did not remember from one day to the next what he had said previously, we must be convinced that in this context reason means something completely different from what it does where Luther speaks about it as an instrument or as being enlightened by faith. Where the context speaks of it as an instrument, reason means the capacity for ordered thought. Here, however, it must mean simply the way that man naturally thinks by virtue of a natural knowledge of law and a natural sense of justice.

Basically, what Luther castigates in his denunciations of reason is man's effort to become autonomous. He knew that Protagoras was neither the first nor the last man in the world to believe that man is the measure of all things. In 1527 he said in a sermon,

> Human nature is not able to do otherwise than to seek its own. What is pleasing to it and what seems good to it, this it considers to be the best; but what it does not like, it considers to be the worst, no matter how good it is.[100]

Human reason in its blindness and madness seeks to give directions to God and to tell him what is precious and good. This God cannot permit, and sometimes he gives us commands that seem most foolish to reason just so that we may learn by actual practice not to follow reason, but to obey his Word.[101] And we must again and again tell reason that it should not try to make itself God's master and tell him what he should and should not do. The Scriptures lead the way here and do it often. But, Luther adds, they have not been very successful in teaching men.[102]

According to Luther's views concerning the alliance between reason and law, it is not the law as such which is evil, but rather man's misuse of it under the guidance of reason. The law does proclaim a perfectly valid way of salvation. The man who obeys it will be saved, but reason is ignorant of man's inability to keep the law since the Fall, and it also does not know that those works which appear most pious to men are an abomination in the sight of God. Reason imagines that because a work looks good to us, that work must be good. But God says that there is no one who does good. We must believe this too, against all sense and sight. Reason does not take into account man's real situation and judges again on the basis of sight and its fragmentary information.

There is a remarkable passage in the *Tischreden* which summarizes Luther's attitude toward the law and also illustrates clearly that it was not the law as such, but man's misunderstanding of the place and function of the law in his life, that he had in mind when he lumped law and reason together. He is quoted there as saying,

> I want nothing to do with Moses because he is an enemy of Christ. If he comes to me with his condemnation, I will send him away in the name of the devil and say, "Here is Christ." At the last judgment Moses will look at me and say, "You have understood me and distinguished correctly," and he will be pleased with me.[103]

THE PARADOXICAL NATURE OF LUTHER'S THOUGHT

It is a well-known fact that Luther's writings abound in paradoxical expressions. This has helped to create the impression that Luther had no regard for the laws of logic or the regular processes of reason. We have seen traces of this throughout this chapter, and it would be possible to string together a seemingly endless chain of paradoxical statements from his writings. Because of this, some have claimed to have discovered a spiritual kinship between Luther and Kierkegaard. But to read these two men side by side is to detect a fundamental difference in spirit. Luther never quite delights in paradox in the same way that Kierkegaard does. It is difficult at times, when reading Kierkegaard, to escape the conviction that the Danish philosopher was quite proud of his cleverness in having discovered the paradox. Furthermore, Kierkegaard makes human reason the judge of revelation. He says, for example, "In a sense Paul too had a revelation, only that in addition he had an unusually good head."[104] This is just the thing that Luther condemns. It is not man's *good head* that enables him to receive God's revelation, to say nothing about accepting it. This comes about only by the grace of God. It was Kierkegaard's "good head" that undoubtedly misled him into what is basically a legalistic theology.

The evangelical Luther, on the other hand, is not proud of his recognition of the paradox. He makes it clear that he had learned this art from the Apostle Paul. He says that in Paul we regularly find such expressions as "I live," "I do not live," "I am dead," "I am not dead," "I am a sinner," "I am not a sinner." Occasionally John also speaks in this way. But

> Paul has his own peculiar way of speaking,
> which is not human, but divine and heavenly.
> And if Paul had not used this way of speak-
> ing first and had not set a precedent by so
> writing, no one, not even if you were one of
> the saints, would dare to use it.[105]

Many of Luther's paradoxical expressions find their root in his insistent demand and constant reiteration that faith and reason must have different bases for their judgment. We have already heard him sound this note repeatedly in this chapter.

> Faith has to do with things not seen. In order
> therefore that there might be a place for faith
> it is necessary that all the things which are
> believed should be hidden. However, they are
> hidden no farther away then under the oppo-
> site object, feeling or experience. Thus God,
> when he makes alive, does this by putting to
> death; when he justifies, he does this by mak-
> ing guilty; when he takes to heaven, he does
> this by leading into hell.[106]

Luther is conscious of how often he himself makes use of such expressions, for he adds at this place, "Those who read our works are well acquainted with these things."

The work of Christ exhibits this same characteristic. When Christ began his great work of salvation, he became the most despised of all men, so far as outward appearance goes. When the redemption of the world was begun, the whole business was carried on in a foolish way. But in the work of God progress always seems to be retrogression according to the flesh.[107] When Christ was in death, he was alive. When he was a worm and counted by all to be the lowliest and most despised of men then he was most glorious and exalted in the eyes of God.[108] All the works of God, he says, are contrary to sense (*widdersynnisch*).[109] In this area if anything is to succeed, it first must fail. When Christ set out to win a kingdom for himself, he went about it

> in such a way that all reason and sense must be offended by it. Even the apostles could not understand it, although Christ had diligently warned them beforehand. So it always happens in all the Bible stories. When God works, he goes about it in such a foolish way that, according to reason, it falls into the dirt, but according to the Spirit it prospers mightily.[110]

The very same thing holds true in the life of the believer in Christ. When God speaks in anger and punishes us, when he hands us over to our enemies, when he sends pestilence to us and hunger and persecution and other plagues, this is a sure sign that he desires our good and that he is well-disposed toward us. But when he says to us, "I will no more punish you, I will say no more. I will take my zeal from you and let you continue in your opinion and do what you please," then this is a sure sign that he has forsaken us.

> But the world and our reason turn this completely around and hold the opposite to be true, that God loves those to whom he does well and that he is the enemy of those he punishes.[111]

Once the Christian learns to judge according to the words of
God, or in other words, when he makes all his decisions and
evaluations on the basis of faith and trust in the words and
promises of God, when he takes his reason captive and no
longer permits himself to judge according to the data
furnished by the senses—then the paradox, at least in this
sphere, begins to disappear more and more. It is a paradox
only because our reason finds it difficult to humble itself
before God and to be guided only by his Word. Day by day we
must learn to

> value ever more and more that which the
> world and reason hate, so that we daily would
> ever more gladly be poor, sick, despised, fools
> and sinners, and at last consider death to be
> better than life, folly more precious than wis-
> dom, shame more honorable than glory,
> poverty more blessed than riches, sin more
> glorious than piety.[112]

But there are other paradoxes which arise, not out of a conflict
between experience and the Word, but in which both elements
of the paradox are Scriptural. And it is here especially that
Luther resists every effort to bring about a resolution of the
paradox. DeWolf says,

> The paradox is an ancient device highly
> useful for gaining attention and making men
> think about neglected aspects of their
> experience. But the paradox is useful for
> communication only so far as it arouses the
> reason of the hearer to harmonize the seem-
> ing contradictions. . . . Paradoxes, in short,
> are useful so long as we look for the truth,
> not in them, but in a new rational synthesis
> beyond them.[113]

To DeWolf the paradox is merely a rhetorical device. He uses the example of a Republican saying that he is a Democrat and meaning by the latter term that he believes in democratic principles. Only under these conditions, he says, could we have a meaningful paradox, and if the Republican really means that he is a Democrat and loyal to both parties, all communication has broken down.[114] But when DeWolf insists that a paradox is profitably employed only when it stimulates men to the use of reason in an attempt to solve the apparent contradiction, and when he holds that our knowledge of God is rationally defensible, it is perhaps time to terminate the discussion concerning reason and to ask him what he means by the word "God." Right here Luther probably would ask DeWolf whether he wholeheartedly believes in the incarnation.

When Martin Luther said that Jesus Christ was man, he went out of his way to make it clear he believed him to be a man in every sense of the term—conceived, born, weak, helpless, dependent, subject to all the limitations of space and time, as all other men. On the other hand, when he said that Jesus Christ was God, he pointed out again and again that he meant to be understood as saying that Jesus was God in every sense of that term—eternal, without beginning, omnipotent, omnipresent, the Lord of all creation. Luther insisted on taking this view with all earnestness, without resolution, without regard for the logical consequences. He believed that here we have one indivisible person, who is both God and man at the same time. Nor was it blind, thoughtless faith on his part to hold such a position. He was fully conscious of what such a view entailed. He saw no way to make such a paradox rationally defensible. He said, "I can follow the idea, but I just do not understand what it means."[115] No one who is "rational" will say that this can be made to fit into the category of what DeWolf calls a rationally meaningful paradox.

This was the doctrine, as we have already seen in another connection, that Luther was sure was at stake in the controversy concerning the Lord's Supper. The denial of the real presence by Zwingli was in reality, so he held, a denial of the full unity of the Person of Christ and of the communication of attributes. Zwingli held that when the Scriptures ascribe divine attributes to Jesus of Nazareth, the son of Mary, or when they ascribe human attributes to the eternal Son of God, this is a figure of speech, which he called *alloeosis.* Luther, however, insisted that this was not a figure of speech. He called the *alloeosis* a "mask of the devil." Luther believed that God, who is immortal, died.[116] And with the Council of Chalcedon he held that Mary is "the mother of God."[117] He said that while it is true that in the abstract the deity cannot suffer, nor can the humanity create, yet in Christ

> the abstracts are not to be separated, otherwise our faith is false. But it must be believed in the concrete: This man is God, etc. Here the properties and attributes rightly remain. The humanity does not create, namely, when the humanity is separated and placed by itself, if we speak of the humanity alone. So, on the other hand, the deity does not die. Therefore in this place we must say nothing at all about the abstract, because faith teaches that this is no abstraction but a concretion, a union, a joining of both natures.[118]

For that reason we can say that God's Son preserves all things, and we can also say, just as correctly, that the Virgin's Son preserves all things. We can say that the Virgin's Son suffers and dies, and we can say just as correctly that God's Son suffers and dies.[119] If reason wants to philosophize and ask, "How can the almighty God be born of a virgin?" we are simply to answer, "I do not understand it, but I am to believe it."[120] Luther does not hesitate to say in all seriousness that God is a servant, and even that God is a "miserable sinner."[121] Commenting on Isaiah chapter 53 he writes,

He is therefore the highest king and the
lowliest servant, true God and the most
abject man, in one and the same person, so
that it is truly said, "This God has no form
nor comeliness; his visage was more
deformed than that of all men." Who? You
mean God? Certainly God is never deformed,
but most glorious. . . . How can this therefore
be true? . . . It is indeed true that these things
cannot be made to agree for those Jewish pigs
who root around in Scripture—no, not for
any wisdom of reason.[122]

In fact, he says, this is an offense to reason.[123] No reason
can ever make things like this agree.[124] Our faith is a
wondrous thing. We believe that this man is God and yet
crucified.[125] And we believe that this is God who was crucified. Unless his death is God's death we are not redeemed.[126]
On the other hand he is man, and yet he has been given
almighty power.[127]

In line with this thinking, Luther was afraid that if the sacramentarians would be permitted to separate the body of Christ
from his deity by denying it the capacity of being present in
the Lord's Supper, they would eventually on this same ground
deny the personal union of the two natures in Christ. In a
sermon preached in 1526 he said,

I am afraid the time will come when our
unruly spirits with their reason will want to
destroy Christ completely and not let him
be the eternal and true God. For they
neglect the Word and operate with their reason. They confuse themselves in their
thoughts, so that they do not know what
they are about. Their brains are addled, and
they are at loose ends and do not know

where to go. That is not the case with the
Holy Ghost. He is brave, without fear in the
truth, sure of his ground, etc. But how this
can be—that Christ is everywhere—you
should commend to God and believe to the
glory of God, even if you cannot explain it
with your reason.[128]

Zwingli and Oecolampadius and Erasmus could only shake
their heads over such "riddles and paradoxes," for Zwingli held
to the philosophical dictum that the finite cannot contain the
infinite. But, as we have already seen, Luther believed that in
Christ the finite and the infinite are perfectly joined without
either being destroyed. The law of contradiction simply does
not operate here.

The theology of the time had sought to defend the incarnation on philosophical grounds with the plea that the omnipotence of God can do anything. Although Luther himself was
wont to appeal to God's omnipotence in other connections, he
held that it cannot be called into court here. For the doctrine
of the person of Christ is in his view not philosophically
defensible. He says that the argument that God can do all
things and therefore can also become flesh is not true in
philosophy. First of all, he remarks that many philosophers do
not believe that God has infinite power. Secondly, even if infinite power is predicated of God, yet, philosophically speaking,
we could not say that the same Person is both Creator and
creature. For as soon as philosophy concedes that God is
omnipotent it can no longer concede that he is a man. For if
God has infinite power, he himself is infinite; and if he is infinite he cannot be man, because man is finite.[129] Not for one
moment, however, is Luther willing to let this form of argument stand in the way of faith. For faith, he insists, is not
limited by nor subject to the rules and words of philosophy,
but it is free.[130]

THE PARADOX IN CONVERSION

The doctrine of the person of Christ is not the only area in which we are faced with unresolvable paradox. The whole matter of the conversion of man presents us with a series of doctrines which cannot be harmonized in a rational way.

Luther held firmly and unreservedly to the doctrine of the complete bondage of the will. Man is never free.

> The will of man is set in the middle, as a beast of burden. If God sits in the saddle, he wills and goes where God wants. If the devil sits in the saddle, he wills and goes where the devil wants. Nor is it in the power of man's will to run to or to seek either rider, but the riders themselves fight to obtain and to possess him.[131]

Man is a captive slave either to the will of God or to the will of the devil.[132] Thus man sins by the necessity of his nature.[133] This doctrine, Luther held, must stand firm against every attempt to make total depravity in any way less than total. He said that he did not want to know of two kinds of free will, one like mud and the other like wax. There is the same will in all men, and this will is equally incompetent in all cases.[134] Thus we are all "necessarily damnable."[135]

However, Luther is careful to point out that the necessity under which the will of man acts is not the necessity of compulsion. Man is not forced to do evil in the same way that a murderer is forced to go to the gallows. He acts freely. He does what he wants to do, and he does it gladly. But it is the will itself and the desire to do evil that he cannot control or lay aside.[136] A truly "free" will should be ascribed only to God.[137]

The critics of what is commonly called "irrationalism" assert that it is "meaningless" to say that God holds man responsible for doing what he does because of a necessity that is built into man's nature, or that God holds man responsible for not doing what in any case he is not able to do. It is virtually an axiom of human reason that a man should not be punished for being what he of necessity must be because of the state in which he is born. It sounds just as "irrational" to say that man will be punished for having the kind of attitude with which he is born and for doing what he, by the necessity of a depraved will, must do. Luther also saw this difficulty clearly, but he refused to compromise either the doctrine of human bondage and incompetence or the doctrine of human responsibility for this bondage and incompetence. Why does God blame man for rejecting his grace when man is born with this attitude of rejection and cannot do otherwise? We are not permitted to ask. If we impertinently embark anyway on a search for the solution, it will only be a waste of time and we will never be able to find the answer.[138]

Erasmus had argued that unless we hold to the freedom of man's will, it will be most difficult to defend the clemency and the justice of God. For the doctrine that man is totally incompetent means, so reason judges, that God "damns those who do not deserve it—that is, those who are ungodly in this way, that they are born in ungodliness and are not in any way able to prevent themselves from being and remaining ungodly and from being damned, and are therefore forced by the necessity of nature to sin and to perish."[139]

Contrary to Erasmus, Luther specifically rejects any solution which sees even the slightest natural difference in attitude between those who are saved and those who are lost. We may not say that the one tried and the other did not try.[140] Rather, we must say that there is the same will in all.[141]

Above all, here again we must take care not to judge God according to our reason. We must believe that he is just, even when he appears to us to be unjust.

> For if his justice were such that it could be justified by human understanding, it clearly would not be divine, nor would it be in any way different from human justice. But since God is true and one, therefore he is incomprehensible and wholly inaccessible to human reason.[142]

This is the highest point that faith can reach: that it considers God to be merciful even though he saves so few and damns so many, and that it considers him merciful even though he by his own will makes us necessarily damnable, so that it seems almost as if he delights in the sufferings of the miserable and thus appears to be more worthy of hate than of love. But if, on the other hand, we could see that God is just, there would be no need of that faith which is sure confidence about unseen things. Just because reason cannot comprehend this, there is room to exercise faith.[143]

Luther was correct when in the closing paragraphs of *On the Bondage of the Will* he said to Erasmus, that of all his enemies only Erasmus had really understood his position. It has sometimes been said that since Erasmus was under pressure to write something against Luther he looked for some obscure point of theology in which he would not be forced to compromise his own views concerning the need for reformation in the church. But the defense of the freedom of the will by Erasmus was much more than that. His *Diatribe* struck at the very heart of Luther's theology. Of Erasmus' attack in the *Diatribe,* Luther said, "You have struck at my jugular vein."[144] The bondage of the will, man's lack of freedom, which bore the brunt of Erasmus' attack, is a corollary of the doctrine of salvation by grace alone. Everyone who desires to vindicate his view of God at the bar of reason must deny either man's total depravity or the universality of divine grace. But Luther held firmly to both doctrines. Reformed theologians often say that a man must be either a Calvinist or an Arminian—that is, he

must find the answer to why some are converted while others
are not converted either in a difference in God or in a difference in man. A true Lutheran can only say, "A plague on both
your houses!"

When Luther stood over against Romanism, he saw that the
rationalism of Thomistic theology drove men to a doctrine of
human free will. Such a doctrine, Luther believed with his
whole heart and soul, destroys the free grace of God by
making salvation dependent (even if only in the slightest
degree) on the efforts, or at least on the attitudes, of men.[145]
Against Erasmus, Luther could write as vehemently about the
sovereignty of God and the monergism of grace and of God's
omnipotence as Calvin did. It is perhaps no accident that
Luther's *On the Bondage of the Will* was first published in America
in an English edition not by a Lutheran publisher but by
Zondervan. *On the Bondage of the Will* has often been called a
Calvinistic book. An Arminian could call it only that, for
Luther believed as wholeheartedly as Calvin did in the total
depravity, the complete corruption, of the human will.

But had Luther been involved in a debate with Calvin rather
than with Erasmus, his argument would have taken a
completely different path, one which would have made his
position even less tenable from a rational point of view. For as
unreservedly as Luther held to the bondage of the will, so
consistently he also refused to limit the grace of God in any
way. He taught a universal atonement. He held that the Bible
means exactly what it says when it tells us that Christ has taken
away the sin of the world. The world which the Savior
redeemed was not only the world of the elect, but it was the
world of which every man can claim to be a part.[146] He says
that we must be on our guard against the notion that the
promises of God are only for the disciples.[147] He died for all
and earned salvation for all. He loves all men with the highest
kind of love.[148]

Luther believed also that it is the earnest will of God to convert all men. He said, "He wants all men to be saved, in whatever condition they may be. Let each one therefore see how he may find himself in that 'all.'" [149] God comes to all men with the word of salvation.[150]

Just as Luther opposed every attempt to find a difference in will between the saved and the lost, so he also resisted every tendency to distinguish between a "special grace" for the elect and "common grace" for the non-elect. In a sermon on I Timothy 2:4, preached in 1525, he said,

> Therefore you may not make a distinction in
> the will of God. There is just one single will,
> for the believers as well as the others.[151]

He expressed the same truth in his *Hauspostille,* a book of sermons for home use. In that book he has a sermon on the words of Jesus, "I praise you, Father, . . . because you have hidden these things from the wise and learned" (Matthew 11:25; Luke 10:21). Anyone coming to this text with Calvinistic presuppositions concerning "predestination to damnation" could easily use it as a pretext for setting forth that doctrine. Luther, however, clearly rejects this view. He says in that sermon,

> Such words must not be understood as
> though there were something lacking in God,
> as though he did not want to grant the
> knowledge of the gospel to all. For he is a
> God who wants all men to be saved.
> Therefore he gives his Son not to this man or
> that man in particular, but to the whole world
> (John 3). He sends the preaching of his Son
> not only to this place or that, not in a corner,
> but openly to all the world, so that one must
> see that he would gladly have all men receive
> it, believe it, and be saved.[152]

Luther wrote a letter of comfort to a man (his name has not
been preserved) who was troubled about his salvation because
he was convinced that God had already elected those who are
saved and that he was not one of the elect. In his letter, Luther
said that the first of these statements is perfectly true and that
all things must happen according to the will of God; but,
beyond that, he told him to forget all about damnation and to
remember that it is God's sincere desire and intention and
command that all men should be saved and made partakers of
eternal joy. Since God wants the sinners who live everywhere
in the whole world to be saved, we ought to find our comfort
in this doctrine and not permit foolish thoughts to separate us
from his love. When God says that he wants all to come to
him, no one is left out, not even the very worst, not even
harlots and rascals.[153]

Luther recognized very well that we are faced with an insoluble mystery when these doctrines are placed side by side. On
the one hand, Luther says without reservation that the will of
God cannot be hindered. He believed firmly in the doctrine of
divine, eternal election to salvation. And just as firmly he
asserts that man can resist the will of God. Arguing against
the freedom of man's will, Luther wrote to Erasmus,

> For if we believe that it is true that God fore-
> knows and foreordains all things, also that he
> cannot err or be hindered in his foreknowl-
> edge or predestination, then nothing can hap-
> pen unless he wills it.[154]

But human reason argues that if this is true, and if it really
is God's will that all should be saved, all men ought to be
saved. It asks, "If God wanted it, who could have resisted
him? Why has his will, which is otherwise almighty, not been
fulfilled?" Luther answers this question in a strange-sounding
way. He says that Christ is both God and man and that
according to the human nature he can be resisted. But Luther

is conscious that that is not a very satisfactory reply to the question, for it explains nothing. Therefore he goes on to say that we really don't know the answer. God has not chosen to reveal it, and we should not tear ourselves to pieces over it.[155] Here we are beginning to deal with the hidden God whom no one can ever know.

If the will of man is always totally in bondage, if there is the same will in all men, and if the same mercy and grace of God is preached to all men, we will never be able to say why in one case a man is converted and in another he is not converted.[156] We know that if a man does not come to faith it is not due to any lack in God.[157] The fault lies completely in man.[158] Why does not God in his omnipotence and majesty take away this fault in our will or change it in all men?[159] We are not to ask. It is enough for us to know that there is in God the will to save all men and that God rebukes the obstacle in man that prevents this from happening.[160] Yet Luther asks at another time, "If my salvation is the will of God, how does it make sense to say that I can prevent and hinder it?"[161] He concludes the discussion of this question by saying that the Lord simply wants both truths to stand.[162]

It is impossible to read statements like these in Luther without recognizing the violence which they do to reason. Luther was also conscious of this, but he noted that all these truths were stated in the Holy Scriptures, which cannot lie. So when we hear these things we should simply say "it is the Word of God and the absolute truth *(die reine warheit)*" and risk our lives for it.[163] We are not to ask our reason how to make the doctrines of the Christian faith agree with one another.[164] Luther often warns that we should not play the carpenter with God's Word. By that he means to say that we are not to cut off anything that does not seem to fit, nor are we to whittle away at it until every joint fits smoothly.[165] Commenting on the command of God that we should listen to his Word, Luther writes,

But if you want men to listen to you, if you
want to edit the Word of Christ and be master over it, if you want to mix in other doctrines to show how it is to be understood, if
you want to measure it out and twist it until
the words sound the way you want them to
sound, if you first want to take it under consideration as something that you have your
doubts about, if you want to judge it according to your intelligence, then you are not a
pupil but a teacher. In that way you will never
be able to get at it or to discover what Christ's
Word really is.[166]

THE PARADOX OF LAW AND GOSPEL

There are many other instances in which Luther sees seeming
conflicts between statements of Scripture. He says, for
example, that the decision of God to destroy the world with
the flood seems to conflict with his command to be fruitful
and to multiply.[167]

But the greatest and the most persistent apparent contradiction in the Bible is that which exists between law and gospel.
Both law and gospel are the word of God and therefore
completely true, but Luther says that we must keep law and
gospel separate from each other as far as the heavens are above
the earth.[168] They are both necessary, and they both must be
used together, but they must be kept distinct.[169]

In law and gospel we see a twofold picture of God, namely,

one picture of fear, that is, an overwhelming
picture of the strict wrath of God, before
which no man can stand. Rather, we will be
forced to despair, if we do not have faith.
Over against that picture, the picture of grace
is set before us in order that faith may look at

it and, with this hope, take out of it for itself
a friendly, comforting trust in God.[170]

Law and gospel are as different from each other as giving and
taking, frightening and making glad. The law terrifies and
makes demands of us. The gospel gives and comforts.[171] The
purpose of the law is to make us guilty, to humiliate us, to kill
us, to lead us into hell, and to take everything from us. The
purpose of the gospel is to declare us not guilty and to make
us possessors of all things. Between the two of them, they
manage to kill us to life.[172]

The gospel tells us that we are just and loved by God; at the
same time, the law, which is no less the word of God, tells us
that we are sinners and hated by God. Of this Luther says,
"These are diametrically opposed to one another."[173] And this
is not to be understood to mean that God was once a God
who hated but now is a God who loves. Luther would not have
said that through the cross of Christ God's anger is changed
to grace and his hatred to love. God's love is unchangeable and
eternal, and God's hatred against men is likewise eternal.[174] In
the commentary on Galatians Luther writes,

> God is not able to deny his nature, that is he
> is not able not to hate sin and sinners; and he
> does this of necessity, since otherwise he
> would be unjust and love sin.[175]

Yet in the *Tischreden* he is quoted as saying,

> This is the greatest temptation of Satan,
> when he says, "God hates sinners. You are a
> sinner. Therefore God also hates you." . . . In
> this syllogism the major premise must simply
> be denied, that it is not true that God hates
> sinners. Here he will bring up Sodom and
> other examples of wrath, but you in your

> turn should bring up Christ, the Son sent in
> the flesh. If God had hated sinners, he never
> would have sent his Son for them.[176]

Sometimes we must preach to men as though there were no
law at all, but only gospel and pure grace. At other times we
must preach the law and works as though there were absolutely
no promise or grace.[177] Luther says at one time that the
distinction between law and gospel is really greater than the
difference between contradictory statements. He speaks of
law and gospel as being "greatly different from one another
and more separated from one another than contradictions,
and yet very closely joined in the heart."[178] To keep them separate and to distinguish clearly between them is rightly to
"divide the word of truth," as the Apostle Paul says.[179] The
force of neither is to be reduced, although both are offensive
to reason. Reason judges God to be too harsh when he
condemns Adam for eating of the fruit of a tree and too
lenient when he forgives all sins freely. Like fire and water,
these two things oppose each other. Human reason makes a
fool out of itself when it tries to reconcile them.[180]

Yet, once we have learned by experience what the Christian
faith is, it is easy to see why both are necessary. Luther says
that he himself was at one time so deeply offended by the
wrath of God as it is proclaimed in the law that he was driven
into the abyss of despair. He wished that he had never been
created, and this continued until he learned "how healthy is
this despair and how near it is to grace."[181] By experience the
poor in spirit learn to know that they are in grace when they
feel the wrath of God most keenly.[182]

The law is for the old Adam. The gospel is for the poor
conscience.[183] Unless both law and gospel are preached side by
side, the people will fall either into despair or into carnal security.[184] The first is overcome with the gospel and the second

with the law. So the poor vacillating heart of man needs both, and in this way the two are perfectly joined in the heart.

> These two contraries must be brought together, even though they are so far apart. For what is more contradictory than to fear and be terrified by the wrath of God and in like measure to hope in his mercy? The one is hell; the other is heaven. And nevertheless they ought to be joined closely in the heart. Speculatively it is easy to join them, but in practice to join them is the most difficult of all things. This I have often learned from my own experience.[185]

Thus these two, which are distinct from each other in the highest degree, both have a place in the life of the Christian. They form a paradox which perfectly addresses the paradoxical nature of the Christian. The Christian's heart is a contradictory heart which only a contradictory message can cure. Luther writes, in a very famous passage in the Galatians commentary,

> The Christian man is at one and the same time a just man and a sinner, holy and profane, an enemy of God and a son of God. Because they did not understand the true way of being justified, the scholastics would not allow any of these contrary statements to stand.[186]

The Christian who has learned to know himself according to the Word remains humble, feels his sin, is conscious of the wrath and judgment of God, and knows that he deserves eternal death. Yet at the same time he lives in pure and holy pride and, turning to Christ, he raises himself up against the sense of wrath and divine judgment and believes that the Father loves him for Christ's sake.[187]

Not only does Luther say, however, that these two, which seem
to contradict each other, fit perfectly in the heart, but he sees
another way in which the paradox is resolved—not by reason,
but by believing what reason can never discover by sight or
sense. He asks,

> How can these two contradictory things be
> true at the same time, namely, I have sin and
> am most worthy of wrath and the hatred of
> God, and, the Father loves me?

He answers by saying, "In this matter nothing at all will bring
about a reconciliation except the only Mediator, Christ."[188]

It is in the light of this distinction between law and gospel
that we must understand Luther's often quoted and
almost-as-often misunderstood and misused statement, "If
our adversaries quote the Scriptures against Christ, we will
quote Christ against Scripture."[189] Those words were written
in a series of theses for a disputation on Romans 3:28, in
which Luther tried to show that justification is by faith alone
without the deeds of the law. The adversaries had quoted the
passages of Scripture in which it is stated that a man will be
saved if he keeps the law. Luther believed this too, but the "if"
involved here was, he knew, an impossible condition, and so he
said in the Galatians commentary that if we teach the law in
the hope that by it men might be justified, we have already
exceeded the limits of the law. By such a course we confuse
active and passive righteousness and become "poor dialecti-
cians," who do not rightly divide God's word.[190] The law
passages are used correctly only when they show the need of
Christ. When they are used in such a way that they make
Christ and his atoning work unnecessary, as though it is
possible to be justified without his unmerited grace, then they
are used against Christ. Luther sets forth his position in this
matter very clearly in the following words, found in the 1538
edition of the Galatians commentary:

> Therefore, if Christ himself is the price of
> my redemption, if he himself is made sin
> and a curse, that he might justify and bless
> us, I care nothing for passages of
> Scripture—even if you bring up six hundred
> for the righteousness of works against the
> righteousness of faith and scream that the
> Scriptures contradict themselves. I have the
> author and the Lord of Scripture, on whose
> side I would rather be than to believe you,
> although it is impossible that the Bible
> should contradict itself, except in the minds
> of senseless and hardened hypocrites.
> Among the pious and the intelligent it pro-
> duces testimony for its Lord. If you contend
> that Scripture contradicts itself, go manufac-
> ture your own reconciliation. I will stay with
> the author of Scripture.[191]

These things will always appear contradictory to reason, but
for the man who understands the message of Scripture and
believes what it says the paradox is resolved in what might be
called, with apologies and reservations, the existential situation. But the basic rule that Luther wants to inculcate and
plant deep in the heart and consciousness of every child of
God is this: in the conflict between reason and faith, faith
must always remain supreme and reason must always be
brought into subjection to the obedience of Christ. Reason,
which always strives to set itself up as the judge of Scripture,
must learn itself to stand under the judgment of the Word. It
must learn to be still and to know that the Lord is God.

CHAPTER V

LUTHER'S APOLOGETICS

Luther's attitude toward apologetics is completely consistent with his view of natural theology and with his denial of every right of human reason to sit in judgment on the statements of God in the Holy Scriptures. Luther, who saw reason as an enemy of faith, would have been horrified at the very thought of reason coming to the defense of the Christian religion. This does not mean that Luther believed that the study of logic and of philosophy had no place in the theological curriculum. We have already noted that he wanted to retain Aristotle's *Logic* as a university textbook.

Nor was he unwilling to have the student of theology study philosophy. He said that it should be taught to the youth of the church, not in order that they might approve of it, but that they might, as slaves in barbarous Egypt, be able to speak with the tyrants who rule over them until they are freed.[1] Of his own experience in the field of philosophical theology he writes, "I had to learn scholastic theology just as Daniel had to learn to speak Chaldean and Joseph had to learn Egyptian."[2] He did not believe that philosophy had any positive contribution to make to theology, and he felt that it should definitely be limited in its use and application. In the *Table Talk* he is quoted as saying,

> Philosophy does not understand holy things, and I fear that men will mix it too much into theology. I do not disapprove of its use, but one must use it with care. We must limit philosophy to its own sphere.[3]

It seems that he would have approved wholeheartedly the view which is described by Casserley,

> that the anti-metaphysical Christian thinker may, indeed, must, interest himself in philosophy. He becomes, in fact, the advocate of a philosophical scepticism which aims at clearing the lumber of metaphysics from the mind, in order to make room for the complete and unqualified acceptance of the revelation of God in Christ.[4]

THE WHYS AND WHEREFORES OF THE CHRISTIAN FAITH

Philosophy has been called the attempt to explain the whys and the wherefores of life. Apologetics often exerts itself to explain the whys and wherefores of the Christian faith in order to "justify the ways of God to men," as John Milton proposed. All such efforts Luther condemned as arrogant and presumptuous blasphemy. He writes,

> The mouth which asks God, "Why did you do this?" belongs on the gallows. And if you ask me, then go ahead and ask in the name of all devils, and I will tell you where you can stick your snout.[5]

This "why?" addressed to God is suggested by the devil, who wishes to search out the hidden secrets of God. Even a human being does not tolerate it if another man seeks to pry into his secrets in this way, and the Lord surely will not permit it. He is Lord alone. And because he is Lord, he has authority to do what he wills, and no one has a right to ask him what he is doing or why he is doing it. God has his own reasons for doing whatever he does. If he had to answer all the questions that men put to him, he would be the poorest kind of God *(der ermste Gott)*.

When someone asks why God deals as he does with men, it is really an attempt on the part of reason to tutor God. This questioning springs from a failure to understand and to recognize his sovereign Lordship. If God will have it so, it must be so, and it is right that it should be so. Beyond this assertion we are not to go. God is limited by nothing, and there are no laws to which he must conform, nor rules that he must obey. No one should expect him to regulate his actions by the laws we lay down for him.[6]

> But one cannot persuade reason of this. Much less can one convince it to forget this profitless, damned grubbing and investigating in such high and incomprehensible things, for it always says, *"Cur? Quare?"* "Why? Tell me why!"

When we are tempted to let our reason ask this, we should bear in mind that God is not accountable to us for his works.[7]

It may seem that Luther contradicts himself when he says that there are no laws to which God must conform and, as we have already heard him say, that God must of necessity punish sin. When Luther says that God must punish sin and hate sinners, he does not mean that there is a law which compels God to do this, but rather that, according to God's own revelation, it is the very nature of the just God to punish sin, and God cannot stop being God. For that reason alone and no other can we say that he must punish. The law, which says that sin must be punished, is not a law that God must obey, but it is a law that God has given. It is a law that expresses the will of God, that tells us what God wants to do and what he will do. God must punish sin only because he cannot be a liar or unjust—in other words, because he is God.

We also ought to be on our guard against all attempts to explain the ways of God to men. If the Lord has not himself revealed the explanation or the reason for this action in the Word, we must take off our hats and stand in awe before his majestic excellence. These are his secrets and his incomprehensible judgments. It is not our business to pry, but we are to stand before these mysteries in adoration. If men murmur against the ways of God, let them murmur. God will not change to fit their ideas of what he ought to be like. If many are offended and leave, the elect, at least, will still remain. If men ask us, for example, why God created Adam in such a way that he could be tempted by the devil and led astray, we can only reply that he is God and that his will has no rules or regulations according to which it must act.[8]

The writings of Luther abound in warnings against this "Why?"—this effort to find a rational explanation for the ways of God, which are beyond all understanding.[9] He even invented Latin names for those who ask this question. He called them Whyers *(Curistas)* and Whatforers *(Quaristas)*.[10]

In the Genesis commentary he speaks of the reluctance of Lot to leave the city of Sodom at God's command. Since God had clearly commanded Lot to leave, he should have obeyed without question, for when God speaks he means what he says and does not jest. But just as Lot hesitated,

> so our reason also hinders and deceives us, so that we are not satisfied with this that we know that God has commanded something, but with foolish concern we also want to investigate the causes to discover why he has commanded it. This curiosity God hates. . . . He wants us to obey his command in simple obedience and to be satisfied with this reason alone, that he has ordered it.[11]

It is very evident that Luther believed that any attempt to "justify the ways of God to men" was a bad business. God's

acts and words and commands require no explanation or justification. They are right and good just because they are the acts
and words and commands of the Lord. To demand that God
should conform to human patterns of thought and to earthly
standards of morality is to presume to lock him up in a glass
cage where we can observe him.[12] From this kind of arrogance
Luther recoiled in horror.

THE WAY OF ANALOGY

In perfect agreement with this denial of man's right to ask
why God deals with men as he does, Luther rejects every
attempt to explain the counsels of God and to make them
palatable to human beings. He also rejects all attempts to
probe into the mind of God or to prove divine truth by use
of analogy. Luther did not, it is true, discountenance every
use of analogy.[13] He took delight, for example, in
comparing his relationship with his son Hans to the relationship which existed between himself and his heavenly
Father. The *Table Talk*, which originated in the family circle,
is especially full of such references. Once when little Hans
soiled himself right after Luther had taken him on his lap,
Luther said that this is the way we also reward our heavenly
Father for his kindness to us.

Luther also used analogy regularly to illustrate the doctrine of
the resurrection. He says that the resurrection of the body is
not a greater miracle than the birth of a man. Reason understands neither one. Therefore the man who refuses to believe
the first should be consistent and also deny the second. He
continues the argument and writes,

> The whole world is full of testimonies con-
> cerning the resurrection. From a tree and
> the hardest wood is born the most beautiful
> flower; and leaves, branches and the mildest
> fruit spring from it. Indeed, because it is a
> frequent and common thing, therefore it

> makes little impression, and so great is the
> sluggishness of human minds that if
> Lazarus were to come to life daily, the
> unbelievers would nevertheless not be even
> slightly affected.[14]

Manifestly, then, Luther did not entertain high hopes for the power of such analogies to persuade men of the truth of the Christian religion. It is true, as Watson says, that in the commentary on Galatians Luther "actually warns us against the view that analogies from human experience are necessarily valueless."[15] But in the same connection Luther says (and this Watson seems to have overlooked), "Of all arguments those are weakest which we employ when we argue from human to divine matters"; and he lays great restrictions on this type of argumentation when he writes, "An argument taken from an ordinance of God or his creatures has validity, but we must use it correctly."[16] He raises the question of whether such analogies are dialectical or rhetorical arguments. While he does not give a categorical answer to his own question, he does imply that they would be rhetorical in nature.[17] In other words, they are intended to illustrate rather than to serve as logical proof.

They may therefore be used most effectively after the matter itself has first been clearly established by Scripture. Such analogies are related to allegories, which also proceed from human to divine matters. It is well known that Luther gradually drifted away from the allegorical method of Biblical interpretation until, in the end, he almost completely abandoned and rejected it. In the *Table Talk* he is quoted as saying,

> Allegories are harlots. They are well-
> groomed, but they are not faithful. They are
> not wives. We should not be quick to use
> them, unless we have first established our
> cause by very sound arguments, as . . . Paul
> did in Galatians.[18]

Arguments from analogy are not only weak, even if they are used correctly, but they can become downright vicious unless great care is exercised in their use. When such arguments fall into the service of the depraved intellect of man, they turn sour and have no validity whatever. In fact they can be absolutely misleading.[19] Thus the Turks say that in one house there should be no more than one master or one host. Using this as an analogy, they are led to reject the doctrine of the Holy Trinity.[20]

In another place he writes that human reason can only conclude from human government that God also must punish the wicked and reward the good, since this is a basic principle according to which human governments act.[21] This analogy therefore serves to strengthen men in their legalistic opinions of justification by works. Both human and divine laws always load the punishment on the one who commits the sin. But in God's justification the very opposite happens. The innocent one is punished and the guilty go free.[22] Thus, instead of leading men into the truth and confirming them in the doctrines of the Christian religion, the way of analogy often leads them into error. In fact,

> the more human reason seeks to investigate and to search out the essence, work, will, and counsel of God, the farther it drifts away from them. Finally it comes to this, that it considers God to be nothing and believes nothing at all. . . . This is what has to happen to all those who proceed without the bare Word, consult first with reason in the articles of faith to see where they and reason will agree. This is what happened to our erring spirits in regard to the Sacrament, baptism, and other points of doctrine.[23]

FAITH AND THE PROCESSES OF REASON

When men seek proofs for the truths of Christianity, it is already too late. "This is most certain, that when we have once begun to doubt and to dispute about any article of faith, we have lost it and have fallen into an ungodly frame of mind."[24] This certainly does not mean, as we shall see, that we are not to search the Scriptures to discover and to ascertain what the Word of God says about any given question. But it means simply that whenever and wherever the Word of God has spoken, then and there we are not to ask for additional proof or to demand a rational explanation of what has been clearly revealed by God in the Holy Scriptures.

This attitude toward apologetics follows from the very nature of the Christian faith, and it is perfectly consistent with the distinctive Lutheran doctrine of the bondage of the will. In the theology of Martin Luther faith is never and in no way an achievement of men. It is always in its totality a gift of God's grace.[25] The conviction and the confidence which is the essence of the Christian faith is not an intellectual and emotional position which a man chooses for himself and by his own powers. It comes about not by a free decision of man's will, but according to the working of the almighty power of God.

Neither is faith the final stage to which a man comes after a long, drawn-out reasoning process by which he is finally persuaded to rest his heart in the sufficiency of the logical evidence. It is much rather a stepping-out into the darkness, where there is no "proof" in the ordinary sense of the term, but only a word of the Lord, which is infinitely better and more certain than all the rational proofs in the whole world.[26] Faith is something done to us rather than by us (*magis passio quam actio*).[27]

Luther warns earnestly against faith which is a work of man. That he calls a "manufactured faith" or a "fictional faith." The true faith, he says, is a complete trust of the heart in Christ. Such faith is kindled alone by Christ. Whoever has it is blessed. Whoever does not have it is damned. Such faith also does not come out of our own preparation, but when God's Word is preached openly and clearly, then such faith and hope, such a firm confidence in Christ begins to spring up.[28]

Luther believed that man is totally impotent in conversion and that faith is worked in man by an act of God's gracious omnipotence, without any cooperation whatever on the part of man. It is a "divine miracle."[29] Luther is sure that if we wish to discuss the question of faith at all, we must first learn that it is "a gift of God and a divine power" and that we cannot believe by our own strength.[30] In the explanation of the third article in the *Small Catechism* he confesses,

> I believe that I cannot, by my own reason or strength, believe in Jesus Christ, my Lord, or come to him; but the Holy Ghost has called me by the gospel, enlightened me with his gifts, sanctified and kept me in the true faith.

In one of his sermons he emphasizes this point again and again and says,

> Beware lest you fall into this presumptuous attitude that you think that when you hear the words you can quickly believe them. . . . It is the Father who draws us and gives the Word and the Holy Ghost and faith through the Word. Both are his gifts, and not our work or power. . . . Faith comes into us without any effort or power on our part, alone through the grace of God.[31]

If men could come to faith by the use of their rational faculties, or if they could grasp the articles of the Christian faith
by their rational powers, then there would be no need of the
Holy Ghost, who alone works faith in the heart.[32] Unbelief is
therefore not due to the weakness of the intellectual capacities
of the unbeliever. Indeed, nothing is more fit to understand
the words of God than a weak intellect. Christ was sent to
imbeciles and for imbeciles. The real cause of unbelief is the
devil who sits in our imbecility and rules there. If it were not
so, the whole world would be converted with one sermon—
and it would not need to be a long sermon either. Without
God's power working in us we can see nothing, understand
nothing, and do nothing in the realm of faith.[33] And if we did
not want to be saved until we had grasped God's promises
with our reason, we would be a long, long time at this business.[34] Even if all the reason in the world were to be concen-
trated in one spot, it could not understand nor tolerate the
Word, and the holier and sharper, the higher and more intelligent, reason is, the less it understands. If the words are to be
understood and to enter the heart, someone higher than the
intellect and heart must come.

> One must come into a different world and
> send reason off on a vacation and not ask it
> for advice. We must silence reason and tell it to
> drop dead and close our eyes if we want to
> understand this. . . . Therefore it is established
> that if a man wants to hear the word of Christ,
> he must leave that donkey [reason] at home.
> He should not deal with the Word or reckon
> with it according to his reason. But if he does
> this, he will stumble. So close your eyes and
> shut your mouth and open your ears and listen
> alone to the mouth and word of Christ.[35]

There is no greater danger in all the world than a highly gifted
reason which seeks to deal with spiritual matters. It would be

easier to teach a donkey to read than to set reason right; and while a poorly gifted man needs one teacher, a highly gifted one needs ten, as the German says *"die gelerten die verkerten"* (The greater the education, the greater the delusion). The more gifted a man's reason, the poorer his understanding; and the poorer his reason, the better his understanding.[36]

Human reason can teach the hand and foot what to do, but only God can teach the heart of man to believe.[37] We have enough to do in just listening to his Word, in which he speaks to us,[38] and in praying diligently for help to understand it.[39]

Luther's views on this matter are brought into the sharpest focus by his doctrine of the faith of infants. In a sermon on the eighth chapter of Matthew he deals at great length with the question of infant baptism. He rejects outright the papistic doctrine that baptism benefits without faith. He refuses just as vehemently to adopt the Waldensian view that infants are baptized on the basis of a future faith. Moreover, he renounces any kind of covenant theology in regard to this sacrament. He says that if this is the best justification that we can discover for infant baptism, then we ought to baptize no baby. Infant baptism without confidence that these infants can believe he calls blasphemy.[40]

For his part, Luther asserts emphatically that babies can have faith. In answer to the argument that it is impossible for them to believe because they have not yet come to the age of reason he says,

> Friend, what does reason contribute to faith and God's Word? Is it not reason that opposes faith and God's Word in the highest degree, so that no one is able because of it to come to faith nor wants to let God's Word hold sway unless it is blinded or put to shame, so that a man must die to reason and become like a fool

and just as lacking in reason and understanding as a young child if he is to come to faith
and receive God's grace. . . . How often Christ
urges us to become children and fools and
damns reason![41]

He goes on to say that children are much better qualified for
faith than adults just on this account that in them reason is
still weak and not yet fully developed. The "big head" of
adults will not go through the narrow gate. Again in that
connection he stresses that we should remember always that
faith is God's work and not the product of reason. Adults
often hear the Word of God with their ears and with their
reason but without faith. Children grasp it with their ears,
without reason, but with faith. "The less there is of reason,
the closer we are to faith," he asserts. What faith does with
God's word is a far deeper thing than what reason does with
it. For faith

is solely God's work, above all reason, and is
as near to a child as to an adult, yes, much
nearer, and as far from an adult as from a
child, yes, much farther.[42]

The less there is of reason, he remarks in the *Table Talk*, the
greater is the capacity for faith.[43]

When the gospel is preached to men it does not require a
"rational decision and acceptance" but a "super-rational
faith." Indeed, reason fights against this faith, and faith cannot
exist unless reason is blinded and made foolish. The gospel is
to lead obstinate and blind reason away from its own light into
the true light, which is perceived only by faith.[44] Faith therefore is not the result of a rational decision on man's part.
Natural reason does not have the ability to see God, but it is
the Spirit of God alone who enlightens the minds of men
through the Word.[45]

ATTEMPTS TO MAKE THE
GOSPEL REASONABLE

Since we have ourselves not become believers as a consequence of rational argument or by means of a rational decision on our part, we should not expect to persuade other men by lengthy and learned disputations. In 1541 in connection with the controversies over the Lord's Supper Luther remarked,

> It is not necessary that we should dispute sharply on this matter, since it is seldom that a man can be sufficiently instructed and satisfied by long disputations, even if we meet once or twice. It requires a good long time to remove such erring opinions and delusions from the heart. For this we require good, friendly discussions and polite, sensible people.[46]

As we would expect from a man who took such a position, Luther resisted all attempts at making the gospel reasonable. Christian theologians are often tempted to do this, and questions like "Isn't it reasonable?" are sometimes asked in an attempt to persuade others of the truths of the Christian religion. Luther considered such efforts to be not only a waste of time, but even positively dangerous and destructive of the Christian faith. Luther considered an attempt to demonstrate the reasonableness of Christianity as a foolish effort to resolve a contradiction in terms. If the *Laymen's Foreign Missions Inquiry* had been published in his time it is not inconceivable that he would have burned it together with the papal bull, if only for this sentence:

> Few men of first class scholastic standing are attracted to the seminaries to be trained to set forth the Christian message so scientifically and reasonably that it shall have strong appeal to all classes, especially to the growing educated classes.[47]

Luther did not believe that the gospel was reasonable, nor that it could be made reasonable and still remain the gospel. Speaking of the doctrine of the personal union in Christ, he says that Nestorius, Arius, Macedonius and the Jews all have reason on their side.[48] At another time he said, "To judge according to reason and our understanding is a certain way to destroy and to lose the gospel entirely."[49]

The gospel cannot be made reasonable to natural man simply because reason (and we must always bear in mind that in such a context Luther is speaking of natural, unenlightened, unconverted reason) opposes the gospel. To natural reason the gospel is absurd nonsense, and reason is the greatest impediment to faith.[50] In the Galatians commentary he says that it is the very nature of all the articles of faith that all reason abhors them and that the gospel is an offense to our reason.[51] In another place he asserts that reason is diametrically opposed to faith and fights against faith.[52] He held that reason and the wisdom of our flesh damn the wisdom of the Word of God.[53] The list of such remarks from his writings could be extended indefinitely.

De Wolf, in his book, *The Religious Revolt Against Reason*, speaks of three basic positions taken by Christian theologians in the defense of the Christian faith. First there are those who believe that reason is on the side of the faith of the Christian church. The second point of view holds that reason can be used to defend some Christian doctrines, but that others, while not in opposition to reason, are definitely beyond it. As an example of the first group De Wolf mentions E. S. Brightman, and as an illustration of the second he alludes to Thomas Aquinas. The words which De Wolf uses to describe the third apologetic attitude might very well be used to characterize Luther's position in this matter. De Wolf writes,

> Not only is it admitted that some doctrines
> of the true faith are beyond all possibility of

> being proved or fully grasped by reason. It is
> further conceded, and even aggressively pro-
> claimed, that some true commitments of
> faith are radically contrary to reason. At the
> same time it is insisted that this contradiction
> of faith by reason is due not to the falseness
> of faith, nor even to the ineptness of this or
> that human thinker, but to the fundamental
> invalidity of reason in the realm of religion.[54]

Luther maintained that if reason could understand the truths
of the gospel, faith would be unnecessary. We need not believe
what we can prove and establish by rational proof and empirical evidence.[55] Faith has to do with unseen things. This is a
commonly repeated emphasis in Luther's lectures and
sermons. He asks, "What kind of faith is this to which reason
can attain?"[56] There would be no need of faith, he says in the
Table Talk, if the truths were rational.[57] Of the doctrine of the
person of Christ he says that if it could be understood by
reason, there would be no faith involved in its acceptance.[58]
The sacramentarians, who denied the real presence of Christ's
body and blood in the Lord's Supper, argued that since Christ
was now sitting at the right hand of God, he could not be
present in the sacrament. But Luther says that we know (and
do not need to believe) that in the sacrament there is bread
and wine. We can recognize it for what it is when we see it
with our eyes. But by faith alone we furthermore insist that
Christ is both at the right hand of God and also truly present
in the sacrament. This does not make sense to us. But we must
remember that if our Lord God had given us articles of faith
which our understanding could grasp, none of us would be
saved. Whatever we begin and understand with our reason will
not help us nor save us. What leads us to heaven

> must be something which is above our rea-
> son and wisdom . . . so that if all the clever
> people on earth were to work together it

would still be impossible for them to build a
ladder to heaven.[59]

As we have already seen, it is the very nature of reason to judge
on the basis of the evidence presented by the senses. But the
articles of faith, the doctrines of the Christian religion, deal
with things which the eyes have never seen, which the ears have
never heard and the heart has never felt.[60] Here again Luther's
doctrine of the hidden God becomes important. Faith is
certainty about unseen things. If there is to be a place for faith
at all, God and divine truth must be hidden. And it is hidden
just in this way, that it is contrary to what we feel and experience. When we think, for example, of the many people whom
God damns, it does not appear to us that he is merciful and
kind and gracious. He appears instead to the reason of man
to be cruel and arbitrary. But it is precisely this that gives us
an opportunity to exercise our faith. So God always hides his
eternal grace and mercy under his eternal wrath, and his righteousness under sin. When he wants to make us alive, he does
this by putting us to death. When he wants to take us to
heaven, he does it by leading us into hell. In such things lie the
province and the need of faith.[61] We *believe* that God is just,
especially when he appears to be unjust.[62] If we could always
see how just he is, there would be no need of faith. If we
would always experience his kindness and mercy, we would no
longer need to believe it.

It is precisely this characteristic of faith that makes it impossible for faith ever to be an achievement of man or a result of
logical argument. More than this, faith cannot be maintained
even in a Christian by arguments from reason. All the articles
of the true faith are so difficult and so far beyond our reach
that no man can hold fast to them without the grace of the
Holy Spirit. Luther says,

> I testify and speak of this as one who has had
> not a little experience. And if you want to

> experience it just a little, then take any article
> of faith you please—the doctrine of the
> incarnation of Christ, the resurrection, etc.
> You will retain not one of them if you hold
> fast to it with reason.[63]

In all these matters the Holy Ghost must be the master and
teacher, or nothing will come of it.[64]

For this reason Luther was also opposed to the use of force
to compel men to believe or to accept the Christian religion. "No one," he asserted, "can or should be compelled
to come to faith."[65] When Balthasar Huebmaier, the
Anabaptist, was burned in 1528, Luther wrote a letter in
which he expressed his disagreement with Huebmaier, but
nevertheless he says,

> It is not right and it grieves me indeed that
> such people are murdered so tragically,
> burned, and destroyed so cruelly. Each one
> ought to be permitted to believe as he wishes.
> . . . How quickly does it not happen that a
> man goes astray and falls into the clutches of
> the devil! One should fight against them and
> resist them with the Scriptures and God's
> Word. With fire one will accomplish little.[66]

With the conviction that only the Holy Ghost working
through the Word is able to create and preserve true faith in
the hearts of men, Luther armed himself against unbelief. If
the heathen said to him that any article of the Christian faith
"did not make sense" (*reumbt sich nicht*), he made no effort to
demonstrate how this could be made to agree with reason and
to "make sense."[67] This conflict between faith and reason did
not disturb him. He was happy that it was there, because he
was sure that if reason once agreed with the message of the
church, it would be evident that the church no longer held to

the Christian faith. And so, when unbelievers said, "It makes no sense," Luther answered,

> Indeed it doesn't. I say this too that it does not make sense in reason and in your head and in human skill, but it must make sense in faith and according to the Word of God.[68]

Luther held that it is only man's damnable pride that keeps him from seeing that the way out of this conflict between reason and the Word is not to be sought in a modification of the Scriptures but in a change in reason. Since Scripture cannot be broken, it is reason that must break. It is not difficult, according to Luther, for men to change the truths of Scripture to make them reasonable. It takes no great skill to philosophize about these things.[69] When unbelievers point out that there are difficulties in Christian doctrines, they ought not to imagine that these same thoughts have not occurred to believing children of God. But if a Christian apologete reacts to this accusation by trying to make the message more consistent with the dictates of reason, he is courting disaster. Paul of Samosata tried this with the doctrine of the Trinity and ended up saying that the Word and the Spirit are not persons, but that the Word is divine intelligence and the Spirit is divine emotion. It is true that in doing this he offered men something that is easy to believe. His doctrine is one that a godless heathen or a boy of ten years can understand, but it is not the Christian faith.[70]

Luther set forth his own position in this matter very clearly. Of the philosophizing and speculations of men he said,

> I could do it too, as well as others, but, thank God, I have the grace not to have a great desire to dispute about this matter. But when I know that it is God's word and that God has spoken in this way, then I no longer ask how it can be

> true, and I am content with the word of God
> alone, however it may agree with reason.[71]

In that same way all men ought to refrain from tampering with
the Holy Scriptures. It is a godless business to abuse the Word
of God to make it conform to the imaginations of reason.[72]
Even if it sounds foolish, what do we care?[73] If a man does not
want to believe what the Bible says, he at least ought to have
the decency not to meddle with it. No harm is done if we do
not comprehend it. And if someone calls us foolish for
believing such things, that also will do us no damage. We
Christians are not such fools that we do not know what it is
that we believe. We will believe God and give him the glory
against all sense and reason. If others do not want to believe
it, that is their concern. And even if it does not harmonize, we
still know that it is true, and we cheerfully take a risk on it in
God's name.[74] By remarks like this Luther gives us a clear
picture of his apologetic stance.

Christians should be concerned with only one question,
namely, "Is it God's word?" Beyond this they are not to engage
in subtle disputations. They should not ask whether it is
possible. If God has said it, then we should be sure that he will
not lie, even if we do not understand the "how" or the
"when."[75]

> Whoever therefore wants to be a Christian
> should tear out the eyes of his reason, listen
> only to what God says, render himself captive
> to God and say, "although these things which
> I hear are to me incomprehensible and
> incredible, nevertheless because God has said
> it and has confirmed it with powerful mira-
> cles, therefore I believe it."[76]

It is not Christianity that needs to be made reasonable. It is
reason that needs to be made Christian.

So convinced was Luther of the irreconcilability of Scripture
and natural reason that he held that any attempt to bring about
a reconciliation between them must inevitably lead to a loss of
faith. He spoke of his own difficulties in holding fast to the
doctrines of the Christian religion when he began to think of
them apart from the Scriptures.[77] He said that if we would
insist on comprehending the articles of faith with our reason,
we would very quickly lose baptism, the sacrament of the altar,
the Word, grace, original sin, and all things, for not one of
these is understood by reason.[78] Of the arguments which the
sacramentarians used against the real presence of the body and
blood of the Savior in the Lord's Supper, Luther said that they
want to measure and master this whole matter with their
sophistic reason and clever subtleties, and he predicted that
eventually it would come to this that they would also deny that
Christ is God, for the same arguments which overthrow the
first (the real presence), also cast doubt on the second (the
personal union in Christ).[79] Luther's prophecy in this matter
has been fulfilled in modern Protestantism, where the denial of
the real presence has borne this fruit.

Consistently, and in the same vein, Luther also expressed his
suspicions about the methods of Erasmus, who earlier than
Luther had attacked some of the abuses of the Roman
Church. Erasmus had used ridicule against the malpractices of
Rome. But Luther said,

> Whoever wants to attack a ceremony, no mat-
> ter how insignificant, must take the Word in
> both hands, and not do as Erasmus, who
> ridicules ceremonies only for the reason that
> they are foolish.[80]

He expressed his concern over the fact that such an attack
would boomerang and strike also the Scriptures. There are
things in the Bible which from the viewpoint of human reason
are just as foolish as any of the ceremonies of the Roman

Church. Circumcision and the sacrifice of Isaac are also foolish things. So Luther asks, "What if these foolish things, which you ridicule, are pleasing to God?"[81] Bainton is absolutely correct when he asserts that Luther rejected transubstantiation "less on rational than on biblical grounds."[82] It is clear that Luther did not believe that reason was competent to judge and to distinguish clearly between folly and wisdom.

SCRIPTURE THE DEFENSE OF SCRIPTURE

Luther knew of only one way to defend the articles of the Christian faith. One of the watchwords of the Reformation was *sola Scriptura*, the Scriptures alone. Luther applied this principle also in the field of apologetics. Luther's basic approach in this matter has been well described by Watson, who writes,

> It is clear that Luther's conception of the theologian's task must mean, at least in certain directions, a quite drastic reduction. He has, for example, notoriously little interest and even less confidence in rational metaphysics—"speculation" as he calls it. His theology is not speculative, but dogmatic. His essential concern is simply to give expression to the religious significance of the Christian faith as he had come to understand it. He does not attempt either to establish its truth on a rational basis, or to elucidate the metaphysical implications of its dogmas.[83]

When Luther was faced with the need for defending any article of faith, whether it be the resurrection, baptism, the Lord's Supper, absolution, the person of Christ, or the Trinity, he usually reminded himself and his hearers of the fact that God has said these things in his Word and that God is the Almighty One who can do all things. We always ought to dismiss reason and simply to say,

> If God has said it, it will surely come to pass.
> Of that I have no doubt. For there stands his
> Word. That cannot lie. Besides, God is
> almighty. Therefore, whatever he says cannot
> fail. It must come to pass. But, as has been
> said, the only thing that is lacking is that
> men do not believe that God is almighty,
> that he can do it, and that he has said he
> wants to do it.[84]

If we could convince a Mohammedan of these two premises, namely, that God has said such things and that God is almighty, he would surely also believe all the other articles of faith.[85] But of this only the Holy Ghost can convince men, as we have seen. We, on our part, have enough to do if we will only set out to repeat all that the Scriptures have said. We do that poorly enough, and our repetition of the scriptural truth is done in a stammering way.[86] But to fail with God's Word is better than to succeed without it.[87]

We shall, therefore, be well equipped to defend the articles of faith against all the temptations of the devil if we are well grounded in God's Word and cling to it firmly when the devil seeks to overthrow our faith with clever fables, which are brought forth out of human understanding and reason.[88] Faith is the evidence of things not seen. It clings only to the bare Word of God, and lets itself be guided by what it sees in the Word, even if it sees many other things which tempt it to look upon what the Word says as vain and useless.[89]

> And just that which nature calls folly and
> from which it shrinks, that faith calls the
> right way and presses through, allows nature
> to be clever and wise while it remains nature's
> fool and buffoon. Thus faith comes to Christ
> and finds him.[90]

Over against the "conclusions of faith" the arguments of reason and experience are always lesser arguments.[91] If men will not accept the doctrines of the Christian faith on the authority of Scripture we should not even desire their assent on other grounds. If they accept them on any other basis than the authority of Scripture, they may expect no thanks from us for that. The cursed devil may thank them for that, because we will not, said Luther.[92] Against Erasmus he wrote that the principles of the Lutheran Reformation can be defended by clear Scripture, and he went on to say that whatever cannot be so defended has no place in the Christian religion.[93] It is the very nature of the Christian faith that it seeks no foundation on which to rest except the bare word of Scripture.[94]

In fact, any attempt to undergird the Christian faith with arguments drawn from reason can have only the most disastrous results. If we want to remain firmly grounded in the faith, we must be on our guard against what reason and human thoughts teach.[95] The only way to resist the temptation by which the devil seeks to lead us into doubt about the truths of Christianity is to hold fast to the clear and definite statements of the Bible.

> There is no better advice on how to stand against the deception of the devil than to hold fast to the bare, clear word of the Scriptures, and think no farther nor speculate. Rather, we ought to close our eyes and say, "What Christ says, that must and should be true, even if I or any other man cannot understand or comprehend it or know how it can be true. Christ knows well what he is, and what or how he should speak of himself." Whoever does not regard this, he will stumble and err and fall. For it is not possible to comprehend even the most insignificant article of faith with human reason or human senses.[96]

Luther's approach to this question was thoroughly dogmatic and authoritarian. The Christian faith, according to him, can be maintained and defended by an appeal to Scripture and in no other way. He held that there was not even one article of the true religion that can be firmly held in any other way.[97] In a sermon at Wittenberg he told his congregation,

> I have said all this, my friends, so that you
> may accustom yourselves and learn to prove
> and defend the doctrines of your faith only
> with the Scriptures.[98]

Such remarks may not surprise those who have cut their eye teeth on Luther's Small Catechism. But in the scholastic, Thomistic theological atmosphere of his time this was revolutionary and sensational.

If therefore the Christian believer wants to be well prepared to defend his faith, he should know the texts of Holy Scripture on which the articles of faith are based and from which they are drawn.[99] In divine things we are not to argue, but only to listen.[100] We are not to engage in subtle disputation in an attempt to prove the possibility of what God has said. If it is God's word, if he said it, then we are to trust it without question, even if we do not understand it. This is a basic principle which underlies Luther's approach to all of the doctrines of Scripture, and it gives us an explanation for much of the distinctiveness of Lutheran theology. Of the doctrine of the Trinity he says that we should not ask many questions about how Father, Son, and Holy Ghost can be one God, but we ought to be satisfied with this, that it is the way God speaks of himself in the Word.[101] Luther manifests the same attitude in his defense of the biblical doctrine of the sacraments. Of baptism and the Lord's Supper he writes,

> You should become a child and say, "I do not
> understand it. I indeed see only water and how

> it is poured over a baby, but I will gladly be a
> fool and a child and believe it when God says
> that baptism has the power and efficacy of
> regeneration and the forgiveness of sins." [102]

If men want to argue with us about the truth of our faith, we
are to limit ourselves to quoting the texts from which these
truths are derived. We are not to enter into prolonged rational
argumentation, but we are simply to say to those who oppose
us, "I do not want to hear your scoffing words and speculations." [103] "Therefore," he says,

> let this be the primary concern of a theolo-
> gian, that he knows the texts well, as they say.
> And let him hold this as his first principle,
> that in holy things one must not dispute nor
> philosophize. For if doctrines were to be
> proven by rational arguments which have the
> appearance of truth, I could find fault with
> all the articles of faith just as Arius, the sacra-
> mentarians and the Anabaptists have done.
> But in theology one must listen and believe
> and hold firmly in the heart that God is true,
> no matter how absurd those things which
> God says in his Word may appear to be to
> reason. [104]

It was Luther's firm conviction that any attempt to defend the
articles of the Christian faith by rational argumentation was
the greatest folly. In 1520 the Franciscan monk Alveld had
written a tract defending the papacy against Luther. Luther, in
turn, attacked the methods of Alveld in the following words:

> To undertake to establish or to defend God's
> ordinance with reason, unless it has first been
> established and illumined with faith, is the
> same as attempting to illumine the bright sun

with an unlit lantern and to find a foundation
for a rock in a reed.[105]

We can prove and defend our doctrine in no other way than
by proclaiming the revelation of God. The reason for this is
simple. The man who does not believe the Word will not
accept any other proof. You will not be able to convince him
by anything apart from the Word. Whatever else you may say
to him will be so much wasted breath.[106] In Luther's defense of
the Lord's Supper, written in 1527, he says that the *Schwaermer*
[his sobriquet for Zwingli and the sacramentarians] want to be
shown the visible body of Christ in the sacrament before they
will believe in the real presence. Luther admitted that he could
not give them such evidence. He said,

> Whoever does not want to believe God's
> words may not demand anything more from
> me. I have done enough if I have shown that
> it is not contrary to God's Word but in accord
> with the Scriptures.[107]

The devil must be conquered with Scripture and not with
reason.[108] In fact, to defend God's Word with reason is like
trying to defend one's helmet and sword with a bare arm and
bare head.[109]

Interesting in this connection is Luther's comment on Peter's
admonition to be ready at all times to give an answer to anyone
who asks a "reason for the hope" that is in us (1 Peter 3:15).
This text is often used today as a call for a rational apologetic
in defense of Christianity. It also was understood in this way
by scholastic theology. Luther, however, commented,

> The scholastics have twisted this text to the
> effect that one should overcome heretics with
> reason and out of the natural light of
> Aristotle, because it says here in the Latin,

> *"rationem reddere,"* as though Peter meant that
> we should do it with human reason.
> Therefore they say that the Scriptures are far
> too weak to overcome heretics. It must be
> done with reason and must come out of the
> brain. From that source one must prove that
> the faith is right. And yet our faith is above all
> reason and produced only by the power of
> God. Therefore if people do not want to
> believe, you should remain silent, for you are
> under no obligation to compel them to
> accept the Scriptures as God's Book or God's
> Word. It is enough to show that your view is
> based on Scripture.[110]

If we find people, therefore, who deny that the Scriptures are
the Word of God we are to be silent and not speak a word to
them. We should be ready at all times to give them proof out
of the Scriptures. If they believe it, well and good. But if they
will not believe it, we need give them nothing more. If men are
afraid that by such a course of action the Scriptures will be
ridiculed or that the Word of God will suffer shame,[111] let
them remember that this is God's concern and not ours. In
other words, it is blasphemous to imagine that our reason can
provide an adequate defense for God's Word. The gospel
stands in need of proclamation, not of defense.

> Whoever believes nothing and denies every-
> thing that we say of God and of God's Word,
> with him we have nothing to do, as it is also
> taught in the schools, "One must not debate
> with him who denies the first principles."[112]

Luther understood the dialectical implications of this
approach very well. He himself points to the apparent weakness of this point of view. In a sermon on Paul's defense of
the resurrection in I Corinthians 15 he says that Paul's argu-

ment seems to be dialectically weak, for the Apostle commits, by scholastic standards, a double error in logic. In the first place, Luther says, the heathen will accuse Paul of trying to prove that which is denied by what is denied.[113] The unbeliever will not see the resurrection of Christ as proof for the resurrection of all men because the first means as little to him as the second. Thus from the view point of the unbeliever Paul is guilty of begging the question. In these comments Luther exhibits a clear understanding of the logical processes involved in theological debate. He illustrates Paul's method by saying,

> If someone were to accuse another before a court and say, "You are a rascal, etc.," and when called upon to prove it simply keeps on repeating the same thing and saying, "It is true, you are a rascal. You have always been a rascal from the time of your conception and birth," one would not call that proof, but empty and useless babbling.[114]

The second logical weakness, again from the unbelieving point of view, which Luther points out in his comments on Paul's argument is the fallacy of arguing from the particular to the universal. Even if Christ is risen this would not be a logical justification for the assertion that all men will rise, for from the fact that one judge is a scoundrel it does not follow that all judges are scoundrels. Nor can we predict a whole summer from one fine day. But, nevertheless, in spite of the dialectical weakness in Paul's argument, Luther insists that Paul's way of defending the doctrine of the resurrection is the correct method of guarding every article of faith. [115]

THE PLACE OF REASON IN APOLOGETICS

After having heard Luther's scornful and vehement denunciation of the use of reason in the defense of Scripture, it is a little surprising to hear him insist, as he did at Worms, that he would bow to the dictates of sound reason. It is still more surprising to find that he repeatedly castigates his opponents as irrational and senseless fools. It would seem at first glance that we are here faced with an inconsistency in the thought of the great reformer.

However, it will become evident upon more careful evaluation of Luther's method that he is entirely consistent. We have heard him say, in regard to the natural knowledge of God, that there is no argument from reason that cannot be overthrown by another argument from reason.[116] While Luther believed that it was ridiculous and downright blasphemous to presume to defend Scripture with rational argumentation, yet he also believed that it was perfectly proper to point out the logical weakness in the attacks made on Scripture whenever the opportunity to do so presented itself. In his controversies with his adversaries he says a number of times, "This reason itself is forced to admit."[117] It is evident that Luther did not place a great deal of confidence in such a procedure, but there is scarcely an opponent against whom he did not use this approach.

He uses it repeatedly in his *On the Bondage of the Will* against Erasmus. He is willing, for example, to give Erasmus a logical explanation of the manner in which it can be said that God works evil. On the one hand we ought to be content with the words of God since God's ways are past all accounting. Still he says,

> Nevertheless in deference to reason, that is, to human foolishness, it is permitted to be foolish and silly and to try in a stumbling way to attempt to offer some solution to this problem.[118]

Even reason, he says, agrees that God works all in all. So God works also in evil men and concurs in all their acts in the same way in which a skilled rider rides a three-legged horse. Such a horse is ridden badly through no fault of the rider, and when we say that God works evil in us we must never understand this to mean that God is the cause of evil or that he works a new evil in us.[119]

Erasmus had quoted Ecclesiasticus, which says, "If you will keep the commandments, they will keep you," and argued that to speak thus to a man who has no free will is to mock his incapacity. He compared it to saying to a blind man, "If you look, you will find a treasure," or to a deaf man, "If you listen, I will tell you a story." To this Luther answers that these are all arguments drawn from human reason, which is accustomed to inventing such wise sayings, for reason always interprets Scripture with its own deductions and conclusions and twists it according to its pleasure. Reason says nothing but foolish and absurd things, especially when it begins to show its wisdom in holy things.[120] This is a rather remarkable statement since it is apparent that what Luther is saying is that reason is often unreasonable by its own standards. It also helps us to attain to greater clarity about what Luther had in mind when he spoke of "reason." It is in reality a good gift of God which the depraved nature of man uses in a depraved way.

Having said that, Luther continues the argument against Erasmus on a purely rational basis, or, it might be better to say, in a thoroughly logical vein. He says that if we ask Erasmus and the papists to prove from words such as "if you will," "if you do," "if you hear," that the will is free, they tell us that the nature of words and the accepted manner of speaking demand this. Luther says that this is the fallacy of metabasis (an argument based on an analogy), and that analogies prove nothing. Therefore, all that reason has proved, if it has proved anything at all, is that reason is foolish. Moreover, so Luther argues, it is by no means universal usage to speak this way. A doctor may ask a patient to do something that he cannot do in order to show the patient that he cannot do it. Parents may also sometimes deal this way with their children.[121] He says,

> I mention this only in order to show reason,
> in regard to its conclusions, how foolishly it
> adds them to the Scriptures, and also how
> blind it is not to see that its conclusions do
> not always hold good even in human matters
> and words.[122]

Reason is accustomed to make universals out of particulars, and when it sees something happen a few times, it immediately foolishly assumes that things always follow the same course. It is evident that Luther saw the inherent weakness in all inductive reasoning.[123] It is also significant that Luther was willing to use against the position of his opponents an argument which he was not willing to use or to allow against Scripture.

Erasmus had used the argument that God would not command men to do what they are unable to do. From this he concluded that men must have the ability to do what God commands and consequently must have a free will. In doing this, Erasmus did not intend to recede from the standard Semi-Pelagian position of the Roman Church. But Luther insists that if Erasmus is right—if the commands of God prove that man has the ability to do what God commands— then Erasmus is wrong and Pelagians are right. So, Luther says, the *Diatribe* cuts her own throat with her own sword.[124]

In the same way he often pointed out logical weaknesses in the arguments of the Anabaptists. Some of the Anabaptists had insisted that the children who were brought to the Lord Jesus for his blessing were not children age-wise, but "children" in respect to their faith. In regard to this interpretation Luther says,

> But whoever has a little reason will see that
> the devil has possessed the Anabaptists com-
> pletely, for they, in the name of all hangmen,
> characterize the children as being without
> reason, but they themselves are not only with-

out reason, but they are completely insane
and foolish, since they do not want to let
those who are "carried in the arms" be children, as the text clearly says.[125]

Luther offers to meet the Anabaptists on their own ground
and to fight them with their own cleverness.[126] In regard to
"believer baptism" he says that we have as little assurance of
the faith of an adult as we have of a child's faith. The view that
only believers should be baptized, he says, is not tenable from
a logical standpoint because we cannot be sure that a man who
confesses faith with his mouth is not lying and deceiving.
Adults are able to deceive us just because they have reason, but
infants cannot do this just because of their lack of reason.[127]

In the *Table Talk* Luther refers to the example of Cornelius,
which had been adduced by the Anabaptists to prove that only
those who have confessed their faith should be baptized. This
he characterized as the logical fallacy of proceeding from the
particular to the universal. Even if it is granted that Cornelius
was baptized upon profession of faith, it would not follow
that he was baptized on account of his faith.[128]

At the end of the treatise *Against the Heavenly Prophets* Luther has
a chapter entitled, "Concerning Mistress Hulda, Dr. Carlstadt's
Clever Reason, in this Sacrament." In this chapter he endeavors
to show that the arguments of Carlstadt are not logically
sound, and that they become ridiculous if applied in analogous
situations. He reminds Carlstadt that it is just as correct from
a grammatical point of view to remove the bread from the
Lord's Supper as it is to remove the body of Christ from it. A
figure of speech works both ways, he says. Carlstadt argued
that Christ must have pointed to himself and could not have
pointed to the bread when he said, "This is my body." Luther
retorts that in this case no mother could point to a crib and say
"This is my child," for the learned Dr. Carlstadt would ask her,
"You mean that this crib is your baby?"[129]

It must be noted throughout that Luther is not seeking to establish the truth by reason, but to show that the arguments of Carlstadt are weak. If they are consistently followed to their logical conclusion they will always end in nonsense. Luther insists that the most irrational procedure of all is to refuse to let the words of Scripture stand as they read.

Another criticism which Luther directed against Carlstadt is one which all those engaged in doctrinal controversy always ought to keep earnestly in mind. Luther insists that the adversaries should be dealt with fairly. Carlstadt, he says, not only misquotes Scripture, but he also misquotes the papists. He should not be so mad, says Luther, as to attack the pope with what he knows are false accusations. On this score, too, as on many others, he applies to Carlstadt the epithet *"unsinnig,"* which might be translated "unreasonable." [130]

Someone may argue that these controversies of Luther with Carlstadt and the Anabaptists and Erasmus belong in the field of polemics and not apologetics, yet Luther himself would have made no such distinction. To him there was no great difference between the unbelief of the Jew and the Mohammedan which denied the Trinity and the unbelief which denied the efficacy of baptism and the real presence in the Lord's Supper. Both, to Luther, are manifestations of man's natural rebellion against the truth of God.

The papists are to be attacked in the same way as the Mohammedans. Commenting on the pope's prohibition of marriage on the part of priests and his claim to be above Scripture, Luther once said,

> That senseless, asinine pope has dealt so
> crudely that it would have been possible to
> lay hold of him with the judgment of reason,
> even if we did not have Scripture. [131]

Toward the end of 1519 the faculty of Louvain issued a condemnation of the *Ninety-Five Theses* and of some other works by Luther.[132] In reply, Luther says that the learned faculty at Louvain argues like a bunch of old women, who say, "It is so! It is not so! Yes! No! You are wrong! I am not wrong!" He complains that they use neither reason nor Scripture against him, but only the feelings of their own hearts and their own opinions.[133] They answer him simply by reasserting the very things which he attacks as untrue, and therefore they are guilty of begging the question. Here again Luther uses an argument which he does not allow anyone to use against the Scriptures. And then, having pointed out the logical fallacy in the university's chain of reasoning, Luther adds what was for them the crowning insult, that this is "forbidden even by Aristotle."[134] In the same way he complains that Alveld had been unable to prove him wrong either by Scripture or by reason.[135]

Early in 1521 Luther published a reply to Mabrosius Catherinus, who had written a treatise against him in defense of Sylvester Prierias and the papacy. In this work Luther sets up a series of syllogisms in the scholastic manner to disprove the contention that the pope is the successor of Peter. Having done so, he says, "Do you see, most excellent Thomist, that the Beast [evidently Luther himself] is also a dialectician?"[136] In that connection he challenges Catherinus to deny one of his major or minor premises.

All these examples make it abundantly clear that Luther is not averse to the use of reason in the area of apologetics. Its value is limited, indeed, but he is fond of saying that he can think as logically as his adversaries and that he understands Aristotle as well as they do.[137] He ridicules the supposed intelligence of his opponents. He holds that most of their arguments are such that any fool can invent syllogisms such as theirs. The Jews and the Mohammedans in their splendid wisdom consider us Christians to be fools because we say that God has a Son, or that God died. In regard to that Luther becomes bitterly sarcastic and writes,

> Here the highly, more highly and most highly super-intelligent people, the Turks and the Jews, teach us that God cannot die and that he has no wife. How would or could we poor Christians ever know this, if these completely superior masters did not show us mad geese and ducks, that God has no wife and that he cannot die?[138]

He goes on to say, then, that it would not be surprising if, wherever a Jew or a Turk is found, the earth itself would jump over the heavens and the heavens would fall down at their feet. How are we poor Christians ever to stand up against such wisdom? What will happen to us if ever they begin to ask questions like the following:

> Who will find a nurse for God? Where will he get a baby sitter? Who will pipe and dance at his wedding? Who will say masses for his soul?[139]

But when they say, "Fooey on the Christians, who worship a mortal God," then we reply, "Yes, fooey on you, Mohammed. They call you a prophet? Why, you are a gross madman and a donkey."[140]

It is clear that Luther did not believe that the Christian church had a monopoly on folly and irrationalism, and he knew that unbelievers could be just as foolish and irrational in their arguments as Christians. While he would never have written a book on the reasonableness of Christianity, he might conceivably have been the author of one with the title *The Irrationalism of Unbelief.* Philosophy will fulfill its proper role in the church when it serves to destroy the "pretensions of speculative reason."[141]

As we have said, Luther was certainly not averse to the use of reason in debate with unbelievers. He warns against the use of reason in the doctrine of justification, in matters of conscience, and in regard to satisfaction, remission of sins, reconciliation and eternal salvation. But

> at other times, whenever you must, outside of this doctrine of justification, debate with Jews, Turks, and sectarians about the wisdom, or the power, or the attributes of God, then use all your skill, and be as subtle and sharp a debater as you can be, for then you are in a different kind of argument.[142]

Such disputations with Jews, Mohammedans and sectarians are possible because many things are clear in the light of natural reason. Not every point of doctrine could be argued on this ground, for there are many things that are not clear in the light of nature. Many of these, however, are clarified in the light of grace. But even in the light of grace not every problem is answered. For a solution to the problems that remain unilluminated by the light of grace we must wait for the light of glory in heaven.[143]

Thus, while it is possible to find in Luther a most vehement rejection of reason, yet he did not deny all common ground between the believer and the unbeliever. Both share the light of nature. But while it is clear that the truth of Christianity cannot be proved by rational argument, it also is certain that the premises of unbelief are subject to the same weakness. Reason always leaves men in darkness and uncertainty.

ILLUSTRATIONS OF LUTHER'S APOLOGETICS
It may be good, before closing this discussion of Luther's apologetics, to take note of a few concrete examples which illustrate Luther's defense of Christian truth. Whenever rational arguments are advanced against any article of the

Christian faith, Luther is in the habit of appealing to the omnipotence of God as the answer to all such objections. We have to remember that Luther lived in a philosophical environment which took the omnipotence of God for granted. Even his bitterest enemies, the papists, the Jews, and the Mohammedans, all agreed that God was almighty. With the omnipotence of God he defends the miracles, the resurrection of the dead, the efficacy of baptism,[144] the incarnation of Christ, the virgin birth, and the real presence of the body and blood of Christ in the Lord's Supper.[145] He reminds his readers that the words, "This is my body," and "This is my blood," are not the words of a baker or a tavern-keeper, but of God Almighty.[146] Reason herself must grant, he argues, that if God is truly almighty, then all questions concerning the possibility of the historical events of Christianity are already answered.

> When this first premise, that is, this ground and chief article stands firm, that God is the almighty Maker of all creatures, then this follows in such a way that one cannot contradict or deny that all things are possible for God. . . . Ask all reason, and it will be forced to confess and to say, "If this is true that God is almighty, then one can posit nothing that would be impossible for him. Therefore here all objections of clever reason are silenced, and the doctrine of the resurrection follows strongly and mightily from the doctrine of creation.[147]

Luther did not believe that it was possible to give a rational demonstration of the major premise, of the omnipotence of God. He specifically rejects this idea and says that only faith can know that God is all-powerful. But he insists, very logically, that once a man has accepted the premise of the omnipotence of God, he should no longer deny any of the plain statements of Scripture on the ground that they seem to be impossible to human reason. To such as deny the clear

meaning of the words, faith says, "You fool, God is almighty
and therefore all things are possible." Carlstadt and the
Anabaptists, although they confess the creed and say, "I
believe in God the Father Almighty," do not really believe or
understand what they are saying, for

> even reason can know that if we once admit
> that God is almighty, then one must also
> admit that everything that God says can and
> must come to pass.[148]

Luther was convinced that only the Holy Ghost, working
through word and sacrament, can bring men to faith and an
acceptance of the Christian gospel. Therefore we would expect
him to lay little stress on Christian evidences. But the fact is
that he does not reject this approach completely. He says, for
example, that the Bible is proved to be the Word of God by
the fact that while the Egyptians, the Babylonians, the Greeks,
the Romans, and many others have tried to destroy it, it has
nevertheless survived all its enemies.[149]

Luther sees one of the strongest proofs for the truth of the
gospel in the very opposition that it engenders. The mark of
true and divine promises is that they disagree with reason, and
that reason does not want to accept them.[150] There is no more
certain sign that something is of God than that it is against
reason and above our way of thinking.[151] The gospel is a
preaching which offends men—not only men of no consequence, but the holiest, the wisest, the most pious and most
powerful men on earth.[152] When the fury of the tyrants and the
heretics and the scandal of the cross come to an end, it is a
certain sign that the pure doctrine of the Word has been lost.[153]

> Paul holds that if it is preached with undis-
> turbed peace, this is a certain sign that it is
> not the gospel. On the other hand, when the
> world sees that the preaching of the gospel is

> followed by great tumults, disturbances,
> offenses, divisions, etc., it considers this to be
> a certain sign that the gospel is a heretical and
> seditious doctrine. Thus God puts on the
> devil's mask and the devil puts on God's, and
> God wants to be recognized under the mask
> of the devil and the devil is to be rejected
> under the mask of God.[154]

Thus it is evident that if our gospel were received peacefully,
it would not be the true gospel.[155]

In evaluating these arguments, however, we must note that
these evidences are entirely Biblically based and oriented. They
are merely variations of the scriptural test of the fulfillment of
prophecy (Deuteronomy 18:21f; I Kings 22:28; Isaiah
41:22f). The Savior had said that his words would not pass
away (Matthew 24:35). The fact that the Bible has survived all
the concerted attacks of the centuries fulfills this prediction.
Moreover, the Bible says that the unconverted man will always
consider the gospel to be foolishness (I Corinthians 2:14). So
when unbelief attacks the Bible and calls it foolishness, it
helps to establish its truth just as surely as the Jews helped to
establish the Messiahship of Jesus of Nazareth by mocking
him on Calvary in fulfillment of the prophecy of David
(Psalm 22:18; cp. Matthew 27:39-43). From the standpoint
of prophecy, the rejection of the gospel on the part of many
learned and intelligent men is proof of its truth, while its
acceptance on the part of other learned and intelligent men is
evidence of its power.

One more thing needs to be said before this whole matter falls
into proper perspective. Neo-orthodoxy claimed Martin
Luther for itself as a subjective theologian. And so it became
fashionable in the theological world to classify Luther with
those who feel that the truth of the articles of the Christian
faith is established by the authority which resides in the

"Christian faith" as such, and that the experiences of faith in some way validate the Word of God.[156] It is difficult to see how anyone who has made even a cursory study of Luther can claim Luther for this point of view. A close acquaintance with the writings of the reformer precludes this opinion.[157]

Luther is far from being a theologian of subjectivity. He rails against *sensus* (feeling, or experience) with the same violence that he displays in his attacks on reason. Experience to him did not validate faith. He was not a subjectivist. While he did not deny the reality and the value of Christian experience, he insisted that Christian experience must follow faith and not precede it. Man must never build on anything that he finds in himself. Nature, he says, wants to feel and be certain before it believes. Grace will believe before it feels.[158] The Christian, in fact, must be on his guard against ascribing any authority or validating efficacy to his faith. We are not, for example, to let ourselves be baptized on the basis of our faith, but on the basis of Christ's invitation and promise:

> It is one thing to have faith and an entirely different thing to rely on faith and to permit oneself to be baptized on the basis of faith. Whoever lets himself be baptized on the basis of his faith is not only uncertain but also an idolatrous and apostate Christian. For he trusts and builds on something he himself possesses, namely on a gift which God has given him, and not on the Word of God alone.[159]

Luther would have disagreed vehemently with the point of view expressed by De Wolf, who writes,

> May there not be such moments of communion with God as to make other evidence quite unnecessary? Yes, there are such

moments. When a person stands at such a
mountain summit of experience, he needs no
other evidence.[160]

Luther would have said that when such moments of experience become the ground upon which we build our assurance
of God's love they serve to lead us away from the Word, which
must be and remain the only foundation of our faith. He
would have said that the devil thus hides himself under the
mask of God in order to deceive men and to lead them into
the imagination that they have found God without the
preached Word. Repeatedly he warns against the sin of
trusting in our feelings and experiences.

Saarnivaara, in his study of Luther's "tower experience,"
writes,

> His discovery in the tower was also a deep
> religious experience in which he found peace
> and joy hitherto unknown to him. But what
> he felt and experienced was not the central
> and primary thing. That was the discovery of
> the Scriptural way of salvation and especially
> of justification. Never was it the primary
> purpose of Luther to proclaim religious
> experience or ideas. The content of his mes-
> sage was the eternally valid and effective
> divine truth, revealed by God, recorded in the
> Scriptures, and preached in the church.[161]

For Luther, *sensus* meant everything that is usually included
under the term "Christian experience." Luther evaluated and
characterized the dominant theological tendencies of his time
in the following way:

> The whole order of the papists consists in
> doing, of the Anabaptists in feeling, of the

Christian in neither, but only always in believing.[162]

"Believing," for Luther, meant simply an acceptance of the bare Word of God and a trust-filled resting on its promises. In Lutheran circles since that time it has become customary to speak of Roman theology as resting on works, of Reformed theology as resting on Christian experience, and of Lutheran theology as resting on the words and promises of God. "Feeling and faith do not stand next to each other," says Luther.[163] We are not to judge according to our feelings, but only according to the Word of God.[164] In his commentary on Galatians he says that we should not feel, but only believe, and that we should by no means base our confidence on our feelings.[165] We must fight against feeling with faith.[166]

These are not the convictions of a subjectivistic theologian. When Luther speaks of faith as a stepping out into the darkness, he does not mean that faith closes its eyes and steps off a cliff into nothingness. When he speaks of closing one's eyes, he defines those eyes as the eyes of reason, and it should be noted that he says that when we close our eyes we should open our ears. The eyes of reason must be put out indeed.[167] But faith has better eyes than reason, and faith can see in the dark. What Luther means by stepping out into darkness is a willingness to trust the Word even though we have no rational or empirical proof for its truth.

> Grace cheerfully steps out into the darkness,
> follows the bare Word and Scripture, whether
> it appears to be so or not. Whether nature
> considers it to be true or false, still grace
> holds fast to the Word.[168]

Kierkegaard and his neo-orthodox descendants have consistently misused Luther's words about stepping out into the darkness. Luther did not believe that a Christian steps out over an abyss where he has nothing to sustain him but his faith. Properly speaking, faith does not sustain the Christian apart from the Word. It is the Word that serves as the solid ground on which faith takes its stand. With Job, Luther would have said, "Though he slay me, yet will I trust in him" (Job 13:15). He was thoroughly objectivistic in his attitude. And Lutheran theology has echoed that objectivity by singing,

> *Und wenn mein Herz spricht lauter Nein*
> *Dein Wort soll mir gewisser sein,*[169]
> (Though "No" may be my heart's reply
> Still on your Word I shall rely.)

and again,

> *Ich glaub' was Christi Wort verspricht,*
> *Ich fuehl' es oder fuehl' es nicht,*[170]
> (I believe in what my Savior taught,
> I trust it whether felt or not.)

and again,

> *Sagt das Fleisch gleich immer nein,*
> *Lass dein Wort gewisser sein.*[171]
> (Though flesh says, "No, it cannot be,"
> Let your Word be our certainty.)

After all is said and done, the whole of Luther's apologetics can still adequately be summed up in a sentence which he wrote into the margin of his copy of the works of Peter Lombard, "Arguments based on reason determine nothing, but because Holy Scripture says that it is true, it is true."[172]

CHAPTER VI

THE INFLUENCE OF LUTHER'S ANTIRATIONALISM ON LUTHERAN THEOLOGY

When Martin Luther died on February 18, 1546, it seemed that the basic antirationalism of the church which he established died with him. A pall of rationalism, sometimes called the "Melanchthonian blight," settled over the Lutheran Church. It was generally expected that at Luther's death the leadership of the Lutheran Church would pass into the hands of Philip Melanchthon, who had been Luther's chief colleague at the University and in the work of the Reformation.

Melanchthon was more a philosopher than a theologian. One of his contemporaries, Musculus, considered him to be "a philosophical theologian made of straw and a patriarch of all heretics."[1] Bente says of him, "Melanchthon, as Luther put it, was always troubled by his philosophy; that is to say, instead of subjecting his reason to the Word of God, he was inclined to balance the former against the latter."[2] In the interest of peace with the Romanists, Melanchthon was willing to sign the Leipzig Interim. In the interest of peace with the Reformed, he was willing to rewrite the *Augsburg Confession*. Already at Marburg the Zwinglians had begun to claim Melanchthon for themselves by pointing out that in some of his writings he had espoused a symbolic interpretation of the Lord's Supper.[3] And to this day the letters "U.A.C."[4] (Unaltered Augsburg Confession) on the seal of many a

Lutheran congregation are an unspoken protest against the rationalism of Melanchthon.

But the greatest disservice that Melanchthon rendered to the Lutheran Church was that, in the interest of making peace with philosophy, he was willing to surrender the *"sola gratia,"*[5] the doctrine that God alone by divine grace effects a man's conversion. He gave a rationalistic answer to a question that Luther had always insisted could not be answered, namely, "Why is it that some are converted and others are not converted?" On all these counts Melanchthon made himself unfit to be the leader of real Lutheranism, a fact which soon became apparent.

Up to 1530 Melanchthon had been conscious of the dangers inherent in a rationalistic approach to the doctrine of the Scriptures. In the *Apology of the Augsburg Confession* he repeatedly called attention to the mistakes of scholastic philosophy.[6] He asked, for example, in regard to the righteousness of works taught by Rome, "If this is the righteousness of the Christian, what difference is there between philosophy and the teaching of Christ?" At another place he wrote,

> Human wisdom looks at the law and seeks righteousness in it. Therefore also the scholastic teachers, who were great and talented men, preached the highest work of the law, and to this work they ascribed justification. But, deceived by human wisdom, they, like the Pharisees, the philosophers, and the Mohammedans, did not see the face of Moses uncovered, but veiled.[7]

But after 1530 Melanchthon receded more and more from the position of Luther.[8] Luther himself sensed the impending disaster. In one of his last sermons he told his hearers,

> Up to this time you have heard the real, true
> Word; now beware of your own thoughts and
> wisdom. The devil will kindle the light of
> reason and lead you away from the faith.[9]

Already in 1536, when he was very sick and expected to die, he had said of Melanchthon, "To Philip I leave the sciences and philosophy and nothing else. But I will be compelled to chop off the head of philosophy too."[10]

The rationalism of Melanchthon has survived to modern times. On the issue of faith and reason, most Lutherans pay lip service to the principles of Luther, but in the application of these principles to theology, large segments of the church which bears the name of Germany's great reformer ought to be called Melanchthonian rather than Lutheran. In the last decades of the sixteenth century valiant efforts were made to restore the church to the position of Luther. The fruits of this effort can be seen especially in the *Formula of Concord,* which breathes the spirit of Luther, and specifically, point for point, rejects Melanchthonianism. It is full of warnings against the conclusions of reason. The great Lutheran dogmaticians of the late sixteenth and of the seventeenth centuries also remained true to the principle of *sola Scriptura* against the pretenses of reason.[11]

But it is not our purpose here to trace in detail the history of Luther's antirationalism down through the centuries. Rather, we want to point out how Lutheran theology, where it is true to its name, to this day resists the pressures of reason. Many a Lutheran remembers how his pastor in confirmation instruction repeatedly and earnestly warned the class against listening to reason in matters of the Christian faith. He remembers too how his parents taught him that in matters on which the Scriptures have spoken we are not to ask how these things can be or why they should be, but simply to believe the bare Word without question, no matter how foolish it may seem.

THE PROPER PLACE OF REASON
IN LUTHERAN THEOLOGY

Lutheran theology has always recognized that reason is involved in the faith of the Christian man. Faith is not an anti-intellectual or even an extra-intellectual process, as is so often implied by those who have a misconception of the Lutheran position. Perhaps some of them are so frightened by the specter of a cold intellectual approach to Christian truth that they permit their judgment to be warped by their prejudices. With Luther, the Lutheran Church, at its best, holds that faith is also in the intellect. Even others outside Lutheran circles will have to recognize this as scriptural. In the Scriptures, faith and knowledge are repeatedly equated. This knowledge involves more than a rational, intellectual grasp of ideas. But, on the other hand, especially in these mystical days of neo-docetism, we have to bear in mind that this knowledge does indeed involve intellectual and rational processes. Lutheran churches in America bear mute and eloquent testimony to their recognition of these claims of reason in the wide-spread system of Lutheran day schools, high schools, and colleges. Lutheranism knows that man is a rational creature before his conversion, and knows also that he remains a rational creature after his conversion.

The *Formula of Concord* takes note of this when it says, "It is certainly true that God has one way of working in man, as in a rational creature, and another way in an irrational creature, either a stone, or a piece of wood." [12]

A stone or a piece of wood, says the *Formula*, does not know or experience what is done to it. [13] Thus it recognizes that conversion to the Christian faith is an intellectual as well as an emotional and voluntary process.

A proper respect and appreciation for reason will certainly thrive in a church where practically every child, in preparation for confirmation, is required to memorize Luther's explanation of the First Article, which lists reason, along with body and soul, eyes and ears, members and senses, as one of the great gifts of the Creator. The most orthodox of the dogmaticians of the Lutheran Church have always recognized that reason has an important and indispensable function to perform in theology. They distinguish sharply between the ministerial and the magisterial use of reason indeed. They also make a distinction between regenerate and unregenerate reason, and they are careful to point out that we cannot dispense with reason altogether.[14] One of the greatest American dogmaticians of the Lutheran Church, Franz Pieper, points out that reason is properly used in apprehending the truths of the Christian faith. This he calls the ministerial (organic; instrumental) use of reason.[15] J. T. Mueller holds the same position.[16] In fact, this distinction is historically commonplace in Lutheran theology.

It is therefore not surprising to find words of highest praise for reason in the literature of the Lutheran Church. In 1897 F. Bente said in an essay read at the convention of the Western District of the Lutheran Church–Missouri Synod (and this is only an introduction to a long encomium on man's rational powers),

> Reason is indeed a superbly glorious, wonderful capacity in men. By virtue of his reason man is conscious of his ideas, experiences, feelings and thoughts. Man can in various ways deal with the rich material with which the senses provide him. Reason begins to differentiate, to separate, to put together, and to set in order, or, as the technical terms say, to distinguish, to combine, to abstract, to determine, to define, to classify, to theorize, and to systematize the stuff which the senses bring to it.[17]

But this is no distinctive feature of Lutheran theology. Outside of the extreme mystics, there have been few theologians in visible Christendom who have attacked reason in its ministerial use. But Lutheran theology is different from Reformed and Roman theology in its attitude toward the application of rational principles in the interpretation of Scripture. It is our intention in the remainder of this chapter to point out how the antirationalism of Luther is apparent in specific areas of Christian doctrine.

LUTHERAN ANTIRATIONALISM IN THE LORD'S SUPPER

If a Lutheran is asked to list the doctrines in which the theology of his church differs from that of the Reformed, one of the very first distinctive doctrines that comes to mind is the doctrine of the real presence of the body and blood of Christ in the Lord's Supper. Leipzig, where Luther debated with Eck, and Worms, where he finally and emphatically declared his independence from the authority of Rome, are extremely important to a Lutheran; but Marburg, where Luther met with Zwingli, and where he wrote, "This is my body,"[18] on the table before him, is also a benchmark in Lutheran theology. Walther says that if Luther had yielded at Marburg, "the Church would have become a prey to rationalism."[19]

It needs to be said that the great majority of Lutherans have forgotten Marburg. Many of them feel that Luther made a mistake when he refused to give to Zwingli the hand of fellowship. Most Lutherans today are not faithful to the doctrine of the real presence. Herman Sasse of Erlangen, one of the leading conservative Lutherans of Germany before the Second World War, wrote in 1938,

> It is an appalling fact that those pastors and theological professors who today adhere to the old Lutheran doctrine of the Lord's Supper constitute a very small minority.[20]

This may indicate the difficulty of maintaining the Lutheran position. There is no doubt that the Reformed doctrine of the Lord's Supper presents no special difficulties to reason. In fact, it is deliberately rational. The principle on which Zwingli operated at Marburg, "The finite is not able to contain the infinite," is a rational principle, a restatement in specific terms of the law of contradiction. Furthermore, his argument that God does not reveal to us incomprehensible things is a rationalistic argument. Calvin called the Lutheran doctrine of the real presence a "perverse and impious superstition."[21] While there may be an error in translation when Hodge quotes Calvin as saying, "It is an irrational and impious superstition to include Christ in the earthly elements,"[22] yet Calvin did say of this doctrine, "It is repugnant to all reason."[23] And any Lutheran who sets out to show on purely rational grounds that Hodge and Calvin are in error and that the Lutheran doctrine is correct is bound to fall into a trap from which he can extricate himself only by surrendering his Lutheranism. Far from being discouraged by their accusations, true Lutherans, who hold Luther's historic position on this matter, are instead inclined on this account to label the Reformed as the "chief spokesmen of rationalism on this matter."[24] At the same time, Engelder, a perceptive Lutheran theologian, says, "Calvin and his followers adopt interpretations which are scandalous even to sober reason in that they do violence to the text."[25]

Lutheran theology might be called antirational on this doctrine on several counts. In the first place, the judgment that Christ's body and blood are truly present objectively in the sacrament is one which obviously cannot be held on empirical grounds. Since reason is always inclined to render its judgments on the basis of the data furnished by the senses, it is clearly impossible to come to this conclusion on the basis of reason. On this ground it is far more "reasonable" to deny the real presence, since at least the negative testimony of the senses would tend to bear out this conclusion—although it might be pointed out that there is always danger in an argument from silence. Yet Luther would have said that just because we cannot see, or feel, or taste, or smell the body and the blood of Christ, therefore room is provided for believing, for faith is the evidence of things not seen. To strengthen our faith in an unseen thing, namely the forgiveness of sins, the Savior offers us other unseen things, his body and his blood, so that we may become accustomed to believing what sense and reason cannot comprehend.

Secondly, Lutheran theology is antirational in its doctrine of the Lord's Supper because it refuses to lay stress on the Lord's Supper as an act of man. Natural religion, the religion of reason, is a religion of works. Man must do something to achieve the favor of God. On this all non-revealed religions agree. And Lutheran theology sees the danger of this *opinio legis*[26] in both the Reformed and the Roman doctrine of the Lord's Supper. According to true Lutheranism, it is God who comes to men in the sacrament. What men do there is relatively unimportant. Even what they believe cannot alter the nature of the sacrament. It is God who invites us. It is God who gives. In a supernatural, supra-rational way, he gives to men his true body and his true blood. In his grace he bestows upon man all the treasures of salvation through this means of grace. Reformed theology, on the other hand, is inclined to lay stress on what man does in the celebration. It looks upon the sacrament chiefly as a memorial meal in which the participants remember Christ's work and as a confession of faith in which they declare their loyalty to the Savior. While these elements are not lacking in Lutheranism's understanding of the sacrament, they are definitely treated as secondary considerations. Roman Catholicism, of course, has made the sacrament almost completely a work of man by its doctrine of the sacrifice of the mass. It may be pointed out here that the moderate Reformed position, which holds that our faith ascends to heaven and there partakes of the body and blood in a spiritual way, still exhibits this same direction—from man to God. While both Reformed and

Roman theology tend to make the sacrament a channel through which man approaches God, Lutheranism makes it a channel through which God comes to man.

Finally, the Lutheran doctrine of the Lord's Supper transcends the ordinary categories of rational thought. It insists, contrary to Zwingli and the scholastics, that the finite is capable of the infinite. In so doing it refuses to apply the law of contradiction, which in itself is a principle so basic to human thinking and communication that if it were generally ignored only utter mental chaos could result. It is the very nature of a human body to be bounded by space and time. To insist that a human body, made up of flesh and blood, is truly present in, with and under the bread and the wine is to ascribe divine attributes, in a very real sense, to something which is not, in itself, divine. To say that these earthly elements, consecrated and distributed according to Christ's command are, at the same time the very body and blood of God's Son, is to all intents equivalent to joining the finite and the infinite once more. Reformed theology, like Arianism, seeks to avoid the difficulty by removing the infinite element from the sacrament. Roman theology, like docetism, seeks to avoid the difficulty by eliminating the finite element. By doing this both exhibit a rationalistic tendency. But human reason, when it is confronted with the Lutheran doctrine, must recognize that violence is being done to its basic premises. But Lutheranism simply says that we must believe the Word of God rather than the law of contradiction. It therefore chooses to ignore every protest of reason. It insists that if Jesus said, "This is my body," then we are simply to believe that it is his body. We are not to explain, as Reformed theology does, why this cannot be understood literally. Nor are we to try to demonstrate, as Roman theology does, how it is possible to understand these words literally.

Lutheranism is conscious of its antirationalism on this point. The *Formula of Concord* warns again and again against the dangers which human reason poses to this doctrine.[27] That same confession frankly states that the Reformed position is "agreeable and plausible . . . to our reason,"[28] but the writers of this confession express their resolve never to be diverted from this doctrine by any "objections or human contradictions spun from human reason, however charming they may appear to reason."[29]

And so the Lutheran Church confesses in one of its great communion hymns,

> Though reason cannot understand,
> Yet faith this truth embraces;
> Thy body, Lord, is everywhere
> At once in many places.
> How this can be I leave to thee,
> Thy word alone sufficeth me,
> I trust its truth unfailing.[30]

This same note is sounded repeatedly in Lutheran hymnody. Matthias Loy wrote,

> An awe-full mystery is here
> To challenge faith and waken fear:
> The Savior comes as food divine
> Concealed in earthly bread and wine.
>
> But here we have no boon on earth,
> And faith alone discerns its worth.
> The Word, not sense, must be our guide,
> And faith assure, since sight's denied.[31]

A similar thought is expressed by Johann Franck, who taught the Lutheran Church to sing,

> Human reason, though it ponder,
> Cannot fathom this great wonder

That Christ's body e'er remaineth
Though it countless souls sustaineth
And that he his blood is giving
With the wine we are receiving.
These great mysteries unsounded
Are by God alone expounded.[32]

ANTIRATIONALISM IN THE LUTHERAN DOCTRINE OF THE PERSON OF CHRIST

All evangelical Christendom, and even the Church of Rome, confesses the doctrine of the union of the divine and human natures in the person of Christ. This confession to a greater or lesser degree always breaks through the bounds of reason and presents it with insoluble difficulties. The incarnation of the eternal Son of God is one of the doctrines for which all evangelical Christendom must hear the charge of "irrationalism" directed against it.[33] Unless something is done to explain away the apparent inconsistency, this doctrine assails the law of contradiction. The following chart will help to demonstrate this:

Jesus Christ is both God and man
in one indivisible Person

If he is God, then he

1. is spirit (John 4:24).

2. is omnipotent (Matthew 28:18).

3. is omniscient (John 21:17).

4. cannot be contained by the heavens (2 Chronicles 6:18).

If he is man, then he

1. has flesh and blood (Luke 24:39).

2. is overpowered by his enemies (John 19:11).

3. grows in knowledge (Luke 2:52).

4. fits into a manger (Luke 2:12).

5. never slumbers nor sleeps (Psalm 121:4).	5. slept (Luke 8:23).
6. cannot die (I Timothy 6:16).	6. gave up the ghost (Mark 15:37).
7. dwells in the light which no man can approach (I Timothy 6:16); cannot be seen (Exodus 33:20).	7. appears to men (John 1:14; 14:9).
8. possesses the earth and its fullness (Psalm 24:1).	8. has no place to lay his head (Luke 9:58).
9. is the Creator of all things and made all that is (John 1:1-3).	9. is a creature (Colossians 1:15) and is made of a woman (Galatians 4:5).
10. is eternal (Isaiah 9:6).	10. is born (Isaiah 9:6).
11. is equal to the Father (John 5:23).	11. is inferior to the Father (John 14:28).
12. is King of Kings and Lord of Lords (Revelation 19:16).	12. is subject to his parents (Luke 2:51).
13. is infinite.	13. is finite.

This list by no means exhausts the paradox, but it is apparent that it will be difficult for reason to tolerate the doctrine of the personal union, that is, the very simple and elementary Christian truth that Jesus Christ is truly only one person, and yet both God and man. Men have devised countless ways of making this doctrine plausible. But where they have succeeded, they have succeeded only in destroying the doctrine. As it took a miracle to bring about the personal union, so it takes a miracle of God's grace to keep it intact in the thinking of men. For there will always be a tendency in the reason of man to separate what is disparate, to limit itself alternately to one nature or the other, as Zwingli did with his *alloeosis*,[34] or to abstract the natures from the person. When this tendency gains full sway it issues in either Arianism, which destroys the infinity of the God-man, or docetism, which destroys his finiteness.

Lutheranism sees the tendency to abstract the natures from the person, that is, to separate the God-man into two entities, in both Reformed and Roman theology. Roman practice, for example, renders divine worship to the divine nature of Jesus, but holds that to the human nature of Jesus we should render only *hyperdulia*, the same kind of honor that is offered to the Virgin Mary. Lutheranism sees this as a splitting of the theanthropic person of Jesus of Nazareth. When Reformed theology, on the other hand, refuses to allow the body and blood of Christ to be objectively present in the Lord's Supper, Lutheranism says that this is a refusal to let the two natures stand in real union and communion with each other. Franz Pieper says of the Reformed theologians,

> They desire to hold to the union of the divine and human nature in one person, that is, to the doctrine of the two natures. When they in spite of this deny the real communion of the divine and human natures, and speak only of a nominal communion, so far as the natures themselves are concerned, then we have a clear example of a self-contradiction.[35]

Dr. Pieper used to speak of the Reformed position on the person of Christ as "happy inconsistency." Thus we have a rather strange phenomenon: an antirationalistic theologian raising the charge of illogicality against those whom he accuses of rationalism.

When Lutheranism says that God is man and man is God,
that God died, that the blood of Jesus is the blood of God,
that man, in Christ, is almighty, and that his body partakes of
the divine attribute of omnipresence, it goes out of its way to
point out that this is not a mere figure of speech, not a mere
rhetorical expression,[36] not an epistemological device, but a
metaphysical reality.[37] When Lutherans defend the real presence in the sacrament, they are intent upon defending the
reality of the communion of the two natures in the person of
Christ. It is no accident that the article on the "Lord's
Supper" and the article on the "Person of Christ" were placed
side by side in the *Formula of Concord*. When Lutheran theology
defends the statement that Mary is the mother of God, it is
not intent, as Rome is, on heaping honor upon Mary[38]—and
it deliberately rejects all the illogical and unwarranted conclusions that Rome draws from this statement. Lutheran
theology defends this truth because of its significance for the
doctrine of the personal union of the two natures in Christ.[39]

An interesting illustration of the contrast between the
Lutheran and the Reformed position is to be found in the
hymnody of the church. When Isaac Watts, a Reformed poet,
wrote "Alas! And Did My Savior Bleed," in his *Hymns and
Spiritual Songs* in 1707, one of the stanzas read,

> Well might the sun in darkness hide
> And shut his glories in
> When God, the mighty Maker, died
> For man the creature's sin.

The Lutheran Church has generally permitted this stanza to
stand unchanged, but in Protestant hymnals the third line of
the stanza often reads, "When Christ, the mighty Maker,
died." Although all the Lutheran hymnals I consulted
contained this hymn, only two were found which have this
revised reading. These two were the hymnals of the former
Augustana Synod and of the former United Lutheran Church,

which since have merged to form the Lutheran Church in America, now generally recognized as the most liberal Lutheran body in America. Most Reformed hymnals do not contain the hymn at all, but out of more than a score that do, only the hymnals of the former German Reformed Church and of the former Evangelical Church, both of which were strongly influenced by Lutheranism, contain the original wording. The revised wording, in itself, teaches nothing different from the original, but in the light of the Reformed position on the doctrine of the personal union, the change is significant.

Lutheranism itself, and even the most conservative Lutheranism, has not always been able to resist the pressures of reason on this doctrine. When the Synodical Conference revised its hymnal in the 1930s, it changed the lines,

> O sorrow dread!
> Our God is dead![40]

to read,

> O sorrow dread!
> God's Son is dead![41]

in spite of the fact that the original German says,

> *O grosze Not!*
> *Gott selbst ist tot.*[42]

But generally it must be said that Lutheranism has withstood the pressures of reason in this doctrine with at least a measure of success, by the grace of God.

The *Formula of Concord,* after discussing the person of Christ in detail, closes with these words,

> We admonish all Christians, since in the
> Holy Scriptures Christ is called a mystery
> upon which all heretics dash their heads, not
> to indulge in a presumptuous manner in sub-
> tle inquiries, concerning such mysteries, with
> their reason, but with the venerated apostles
> simply to believe, to close the eyes of their
> reason, and bring into captivity their under-
> standing to the obedience of Christ,[43] 2 Cor.
> 10:5, and to take comfort, and hence to
> rejoice without ceasing in the fact that our
> flesh and blood is placed so high at the right
> hand of the majesty and almighty power of
> God. Thus we shall assuredly find constant
> consolation in every adversity, and remain
> well guarded from pernicious error.[44]

ANTIRATIONALISM IN THE LUTHERAN DOCTRINE OF CONVERSION

The Lutheran doctrine of conversion also contains antirational factors. Lutheranism, where it remains true to the principles of the man who wrote the *De Servo Arbitrio* (*On the Bondage
of the Will*), teaches that man has no free will in conversion. It
subscribes without reservation to the doctrine of the total
depravity of man. Man is not only "sick unto death," but he
is actually and completely dead in spiritual things. George
Stoeckhardt, one of the greatest exegetes in the history of
American Lutheranism, describes the natural state of man in
these words,

> Whenever God through the gospel offers man
> grace and salvation, man not only lacks the
> ability to believe and to accept what is offered,
> but he also willfully and maliciously resists if
> he is not enlightened and controlled by the
> Spirit of God . . . this inability, this disobedi-
> ence, this malicious resistance, continues to

the very moment in which that person is enlightened, converted, and regenerated.[45]

The Lutheran Confessions specifically reject the teaching that man before conversion still has enough spiritual capacity remaining in his nature that he is "able to prepare himself to a certain extent for grace, and to assent, although feebly."[46] The *Formula* says that man is so corrupt and blinded that

> in spiritual and divine things the intellect, heart, and will of the unregenerate man are utterly unable, by their own natural powers to understand, believe, accept, think, will, begin, effect, do, work, or concur in working any-thing, but they are entirely dead to what is good, and corrupt, so that in man's nature since the Fall, before regeneration, there is not the least spark of spiritual power remain-ing, nor present, by which, of himself, he can prepare himself for God's grace, or accept the offered grace, nor be capable of it for and of himself, or apply or accommodate himself thereto, or by his own powers be able of him-self, as of himself, to aid, do, work, or concur in working anything towards his conversion, either wholly, or half, or in any, even the least or most inconsiderable part.[47]

It would be difficult to see how the doctrine of total depravity could be stated with greater force and clarity. This view, says the *Formula*, is "contrary to proud reason and philosophy."[48] And W. H. Wente writes,

> This Scriptural doctrine has ever been a stumbling block to the reason of man. The history of human thought and philosophy

and the history of Christian doctrine are full
of examples of philosophers and teachers of
the Church who attempted to find other def-
initions of this basic human nature.[49]

The Lutheran Church holds that all men are in this state.[50] All
are equally impotent. The Lutheran Confessions often reject
the view that there is some difference in men which accounts
for the conversion of some and the non-conversion of others.
The *Formula of Concord*, for example, specifically warns against
the idea that some men prior to conversion are willing to be
converted and that others are not willing to be converted. All
are unwilling and resist every effort to bring them to Christ in
faith.[51] On the other hand, it must be said that the convert is
not compelled or forced to come to Christ as a criminal is
forced to the gallows. Conversion is the act of God by which
he works a change in man's will. The willingness to be saved
through Christ is not a prerequisite for conversion, but it is the
result of the operation of God in the act of conversion.

All Lutherans, at least all Lutheran theologians who subscribe
to all the Lutheran Confessions, by their very confessional
oath turn their backs on Melanchthon's suggestion of a *facultas
applicandi se ad gratiam* (capacity to be receptive to God's grace).[52]
In other words, any Lutheran pastor who teaches that there is
a willingness or even a capacity for willingness in man prior to
conversion makes himself guilty of perjury. True Lutheranism
denies to man even a *facultas non resistendi* (capacity for being
passive),[53] and it rejects the idea that there is in some a lesser
resistance prior to conversion. There is no difference, then, in
the spiritual condition in which various men find themselves
by nature. Here Lutheranism agrees with Calvin—but because
human reason cannot see how such a position can be held
without at the same time holding to a view of limited atonement or irresistible grace, those who are loyal to the Lutheran
Confessions on this point are often accused of Calvinism by
apostasizing Lutherans.

On the other hand, every Lutheran loyal to the Confessions emphatically defends the universal will of grace. Lutheranism holds that God earnestly desires the salvation of every man. The Confessions say, "It is not God's will that any should be damned but that all men should be converted to him and be saved eternally."[54] That the saving grace of God is universal is an axiom which is proclaimed by every true Lutheran,[55] and by practically every one who bears the Lutheran name. This is a doctrine which has seldom, if ever, become the subject of controversy within the Lutheran Church. Some Lutherans have drawn from it the seemingly logical but scripturally unwarranted and untenable doctrine of universalism, but the doctrine itself is so universally accepted in the Lutheran Church that it would be almost unthinkable that a man should call himself a Lutheran and not accept the doctrines of universal atonement, universal reconciliation, and universal grace. For some strange reason, however, some Lutherans have difficulty with the concept of universal justification. Since the Bible equates reconciliation with the non-imputation of sin (2 Corinthians 5:19f) this difficulty is hard to account for. But in any case, the danger to Lutheranism in this doctrine has never come so much from Calvinism as from Arminianism.

The doctrine that God will have all men to be saved presents us, of course, with a rational difficulty. For if God is almighty and has done whatsoever he has pleased, there are only two possible rational conclusions: either all men must necessarily be saved, or else one of the contentions must be modified in some way. Either God is not almighty, reason says, or if he is indeed sovereign, he cannot truly, in the fullest sense of the term, wish to convert all, or else all would be converted.

Universalism is rejected by all true Lutherans, as it is rejected by all of evangelical Christendom. But Lutheranism sets itself just as vigorously against any distinction between a "special grace" and a "common grace" of God, or between

an "efficacious grace" and a "non-efficacious grace."[56]
Theodore Hoyer says, "This does not satisfy our reason, nor
those who prefer to follow reason rather than Scripture."[57]

The problem which here faces Lutheran theology may be
graphically represented by the following diagrams. The figures
on the arrows represent pounds of thrust, but they have no
significance except to show relationships.

The will of God which wills   The will of man which
the conversion of man: resists conversion:

Calvinism

A ——————— 110 ——→   ←—— 100 ——————— A
B ——————— 90 ——→   ←—— 100 ——————— B

A is saved and B is lost, and it is easy to see why this should
be. There is a difference in the will of God.

Arminianism, Semi-Pelagianism, Synergism

A ——————— 100 ——→   ←—— 110 ——————— A
B ——————— 100 ——→   ←—— 90 ——————— B

In this case, A is lost and B is saved, and it is easy to see why
this should be. There is a difference in the will of man.

True Lutheranism

A ——————— 100 ——→   ←—— 100 ——————— A
B ——————— 100 ——→   ←—— 100 ——————— B

All men are totally depraved and there is no difference in man.
God is equally gracious to all and there is no difference in
God's will. Yet A is lost and B is saved, and there is no conceiv-
able reason why this should be so.

The Lutheran view could also be diagrammed in various ways
so long as the grace of God remains the same for all men and
the resistance to grace on the part of man remains equal, e.g.,

A ——————— 110 ——→   ←—— 90 ——————— A
B ——————— 110 ——→   ←—— 90 ——————— B

In this case reason would say that all would be saved.

or

A ——————— 100 ——→   ←——— 110 ——————— A
B ——————— 100 ——→   ←——— 110 ——————— B

In this case it would appear that all should be lost.

This doctrine has maintained itself only with difficulty in the Lutheran Church. It is the doctrine which Melanchthon surrendered. Synergism, the doctrine that man cooperates, even if only in the slightest degree, in his conversion, was Melanchthon's solution to this difficulty, and most modern Lutherans follow his lead. But true historic Lutheranism holds that synergism is "the answer of reason."[58] Yet true Lutheranism just as vehemently rejects every proposition which would establish either a "special grace" or an "irresistible grace" for the elect. In so doing it finds itself in a rationally impossible dilemma.

Because it is convinced that this is the teaching of Scripture, which does not explain the mystery, Lutheranism has simply resolved not to explain it either.

ANTIRATIONALISM IN THE LUTHERAN DOCTRINE OF ELECTION

Everyone concedes that the doctrine of election is difficult for human reason. It has certain features which exhibit a marked similarity to the philosophical conundrum of the relationship between divine providence and human freedom. But in addition to this general difficulty, the Lutheran doctrine of election presents us with a situation which appears once more to overthrow the law of contradiction. The problem here is much like the one we have just dealt with in the doctrine of conversion. In fact, Lutherans have always said that an error in election will always lead to an error in conversion and vice versa. Therefore we shall not discuss this matter in detail but only point out the crux of the problem.

Confessional Lutheran theology teaches a particular election. The eternal election of God, says the *Formula of Concord,* extends only over the children of God.[59] This election is a cause of man's conversion and of his final salvation.[60]

But side by side with the doctrine of a particular election, the doctrine of universal grace is maintained without any modification.[61] It would seem that if God's eternal decision to save a particular man is a cause of his conversion and perseverance, and if God earnestly desires the salvation of all, then all men should be elect and saved. Yet such is not the case. The Lutheran Confessions, in introducing the doctrine of universal grace into the discussion of predestination, preface this move with the remark, "Of this we should not judge according to our reason."[62] *The Brief Statement* of the Lutheran Church–Missouri Synod, which all synods of the former Synodical Conference recognized as orthodox, says of these two doctrines, "Blind reason indeed declares these two truths to be contradictory; but we impose silence on our reason."[63] Thus Lutheranism sets itself against any decree of double election, and it specifically denies that the non-election of men is a cause of their damnation.[64]

Some have sought another way out of the difficulty. As in the doctrine of conversion, so also here the theologians who hold to universal grace look for a solution to the problem in a difference in man. But this way is not open to Lutheranism. There is in man no cause of his election.[65] There is no greater merit in the elect which caused God to predestine and to save them. *The Brief Statement* says,[66]

> We reject as an anti-Scriptural error the
> doctrine that not alone the grace of God
> and the merit of Christ are the cause of the
> election of grace, but that God has, in addi-
> tion, found or regarded something good *in
> us* which prompted Him to elect us, this
> being variously designated as "good works,"
> "right conduct," "proper self-determination"
> "refraining from wilful resistance," etc. Nor
> does Holy Scripture know of an election
> "by foreseen faith," "in view of faith," as
> though the faith of the elect were to be
> placed before their election; but according
> to Scripture the faith which the elect have
> in time belongs to the spiritual blessings
> with which God has endowed them by His
> eternal election.[67]

But if there is nothing involved here except God's free grace
and if all men are in equal guilt, there is no reasonable answer
to the question of why some are saved and others lost.
Calvin's doctrine of election may be a *decretum horribile,* but it
makes human sense. Synergism and Arminianism and
Semi-pelagianism may destroy salvation by grace alone, but
they too make human sense. Theodore Graebner wrote,

> You have no longer an irrational element in
> this doctrine if those who are lost are under
> a decree which from everlasting consigned
> them to perdition; and you have also elimi-
> nated the unreasonable factor if you assume
> that some men conduct themselves with
> greater willingness under the call of grace.[68]

Carnell, in his *Introduction to Christian Apologetics,* makes the law
of contradiction the final test of truth, even religious truth.
The contrast between that point of view and that held by

Lutheran theology becomes patent when we hear Theodore
Graebner close his discussion of the relation between the
doctrine of particular election and the teaching of universal
grace with these words,

> Though acknowledging the truth of both
> propositions in each of these statements
> amounts to saying that both opposites of two
> contradictory judgments are true, that a fun-
> damental law of thought therefore is violated,
> that the thing is irrational, unreasonable—
> though such tremendous assumptions are
> involved in accepting the doctrine of the elec-
> tion of grace and that of full human respon-
> sibility, we should not be dismayed by the
> necessity of such an acknowledgment. By
> making it, we simply acknowledge a limita-
> tion of human reason which is arrived at *by the*
> *most rigid logical procedure* and is a clear doctrine
> of the inspired Word.[69]

ANTIRATIONALISM IN THE LUTHERAN
DOCTRINE OF PRESERVATION

The doctrine of preservation in the faith, as it is taught in the
Lutheran Church, confronts us with another apparent contradiction. This doctrine too illustrates very clearly how Lutheran
theology differs from that of Rome, on the one hand, and that
of Geneva, on the other, in the matter of dealing with seeming
contradictions. The very terminology employed is significant.
What Calvinism calls the perseverance of the saints, a term
which lays stress on the activity of the believer, Lutheranism
calls preservation in the faith, a term which lays emphasis on
the work of God.

The Scriptures present us with two sets of passages in this
doctrine, which reason finds difficult to harmonize. In the

following columns we have arranged them in juxtaposition to show how they stand in sharp contrast to each other.

Statements of Scripture in which God promises to preserve us in the faith:

Statements of Scripture which warn us against falling from the faith:

1. God is faithful; he will not let you be tempted beyond what you can bear (I Corinthians 10:13).

1. So, if you think you are standing firm, be careful that you don't fall! (I Corinthians 10:12).

2. No one can snatch them out of my hand (John 10:28).

2. They believe for a while, but in the time of testing they fall away (Luke 8:13).

3. No one can snatch them out of my Father's hand (John 10:29).

3. Some have rejected these and so have shipwrecked their faith (I Timothy 1:19).

4. I . . . am convinced that he is able to guard what I have entrusted to him for that day (2 Timothy 1:12).

4. . . . so that after I have preached to others, I myself will not be disqualified for the prize (I Corinthians 9:27).

5. He who began a good work in you will carry it on to completion until the day of Christ Jesus (Philippians 1:6).

5. It is impossible for those who have once been enlightened . . . if they fall away, to be brought back to repentance (Hebrews 6:4-6).

6. It is God who works in you to will and to act according to his good purpose (Philippians 2:13).

6. Continue to work out your salvation with fear and trembling (Philippians 2:12).

7. He will keep you strong
to the end, so that you
will be blameless on the
day of our Lord Jesus
Christ
(I Corinthians 1:8).

7. Do not be arrogant, but
be afraid. For if God
did not spare the natural
branches, he will not
spare you either. . . .
Continue in his kind-
ness. Otherwise, you
also will be cut off
(Romans 11:20-22).

The promises in the first column are promises of God. All the promises of God are to be believed. Not to believe them would be to call God a liar. The believing child of God, reading these promises, should be convinced that he will never fall away, that God will not suffer him to be tempted above that he is able, that no man shall ever pluck him out of his Savior's hand, that no creature shall be able to separate him from the Father's love, that the Spirit of God will complete the work which he has begun in him.

But on the other hand, the warnings in the second column are warnings of God. All the warnings of God are to be observed with care. God does not jest. His words should be taken at their face value. And the believing child of God who takes these warnings seriously will be sure that he is in constant danger of falling away from the faith, that he may be a cast-away, that he may make shipwreck of the faith, for he is not one whit better than Hymenaeus and Alexander, he is not stronger than Peter, he is no less subject to temptation than David, he is no wiser than Solomon, he is no less attracted by the world than Demas. So he lives in fear and trembling.

It is clear we are here dealing with a rational difficulty. Calvinism looks at the first column and draws from it the doctrine of the perseverance of the saints. "Once a believer, always a believer," says the Calvinist. The passages in the second column are either ignored or else they are interpreted in such a way that they are made to agree with the axiom, "Once converted, always converted." A Lutheran finds difficulty in seeing how one can thus interpret the words of Jesus regarding those who "for a while believe and in time of temptation fall away." But in pursuing its course, it must be said, Calvinism remains true to the law of contradiction. It holds that as long as there is a real possibility of falling away, there can be no complete and perfect assurance of perseverance.

The Roman Church, on the other hand, characterizes all certainty of salvation as proud presumption. When the passages in the first column are held before them, they respond that some men may have a special revelation from God. Only they can be sure of their salvation. But the ordinary Christian has no such assurance, and he can have no such assurance. "Let him that thinketh he standeth," they say, "take heed lest he fall." We must live in fear and trembling all our lives and hope that we may be able to overcome. Only if we look at the warnings of God, will we be inclined to avoid carelessness and indifference in our Christian living. Romanism holds that if men are not kept in fear, they will be led into carnal security and will fall away.

How Lutheranism deals with this question is illustrated in a few words in Luther's great battle-hymn,

> With might of ours can naught be done;
> Soon were our loss effected.
> But for us fights the Valiant One,
> Whom God himself elected.

And Hans Brorson has set forth the Lutheran position in this matter beautifully in his great hymn of fear and faith,

> I walk in danger all the way.
> The thought shall never leave me

That Satan, who has marked his prey,
Is plotting to deceive me.
This foe with hidden snares
May seize me unawares
If e'er I fail to watch and pray.
I walk in danger all the way.

I pass through trials all the way,
With sin and ills contending;
In patience I must bear each day
The cross of God's own sending.
Oft in adversity
I know not where to flee;
When storms of woe my soul dismay,
I pass through trials all the way.

Death doth pursue me all the way,
Nowhere I rest securely;
He comes by night, he comes by day,
And takes his prey most surely.
A failing breath, and I
In death's cold grasp may lie
To face eternity for aye.
Death doth pursue me all the way.

It is evident that Brorson had read the Bible passages in the
second column and had taken them to heart. He knew what it
meant to live in fear and trembling. But this is only the first
half of the hymn. He continues,

I walk with angels all the way,
They shield me and befriend me;
All Satan's power is held at bay
When heavenly hosts attend me;
They are my sure defense,
All fear and sorrow, hence!
Unharmed by foes, do what they may,
I walk with angels all the way.

> I walk with Jesus all the way,
> His guidance never fails me;
> Within his wounds I find a stay
> When Satan's power assails me;
> And by his footsteps led,
> My path I safely tread.
> In spite of ills that threaten may,
> I walk with Jesus all the way.
>
> My walk is heavenward all the way;
> Await, my soul, the morrow,
> When thou shalt find release for aye
> From all thy sin and sorrow.
> All worldly pomp, begone!
> To heaven I now press on.
> For all the world I would not stay;
> My walk is heavenward all the way.[70]

It is evident, too, that in the midst of fear and danger he walked in Christian assurance of salvation.

Rationally, it is difficult to reconcile these two attitudes. Reason finds it impossible to see how the man who is convinced that he can fall, that he may fall, that he is in great danger of falling away throughout his earthly life, can also be perfectly sure that he will never fall away.

One answer that Lutheranism gives is that the contradictory heart of man needs a contradictory doctrine. The heart of man, desperately wicked still even in the converted Christian, is inclined to become proud. Like Peter, it is inclined to say, "Though all should be offended because of you, yet I will never be offended" (Matthew 26:33). Like an immature teenager, it responds to the expressed concern over its salvation with, "Don't worry, mother. I can take care of myself." To convince man that he cannot take care of himself, to make him realize that by himself he is lost, that he should never become careless and indifferent in his faith and life, the Lord has given us these serious and earnest warnings which mean exactly what they say and are not to be changed or modified in any way.

But the heart of man is also a timid, quaking heart, which so often needs reassurance. When its feet have slipped into the slough of despond, there is only one way that it can be helped. Man's extremity is God's opportunity. When I am weak, then am I strong. For when I know that I cannot remain faithful, that I cannot persevere, for I am frail and helpless, then the Lord comes with the blessed assurance that no man shall pluck me out of his hand. And so, every day, the Christian, as long as he remembers and believes the promises, will be sure that he will never fall away.

There is no logic that avails here. We must simply hear and believe—believe it when God tells us that we are in danger, believe it when God tells us that we are in no danger. Theodore Engelder says that when reason tells us that,

> according to the laws of psychology, fear, real fear, and trust, real trust, cannot be in the same heart, that consequently either those passages of Scripture which warn against defection or those passages (preferably those) which guarantee against defection must be eliminated or modified, we say: A plague upon your psychology.[71]

Thus the Christian must learn to live in constant tension between these two. When he begins to lean over to the left, toward pride and presumption and confidence in the strength of his faith, and to trust in his own character, then the warnings against apostasy, the Savior's, "Watch and pray, lest ye enter into temptation," pushes him upright once more. But usually man, even the Christian man, whose heart is never fully what it ought to be, begins then to lean over to the right—he becomes afraid and begins to doubt that he will ever make it to the gates of the heavenly city. Once again the Savior comes and stands on the other side to support him and to push him upright once more with his promise, "Do not fear, for I am with you; do not be dismayed, for I am your God" (Isaiah 41:10). And he knows that when his pilgrimage comes to an end, "all the trumpets" will be blowing "for him on the other side."

ANTIRATIONALISM IN THE LUTHERAN DOCTRINE OF LAW AND GOSPEL

As the last exhibit in the catalog of Lutheran antirationalisms, we turn now to an apparent contradiction which is both one of the most difficult and one of the simplest of all. It is the distinction between law and gospel. All the previous discussion is but a concrete demonstration of this fundamental distinction. Luther held that a theologian worthy of the name must know how to divide the word of truth, that is, he must understand the basic difference between these two doctrines. The chief founder of the Lutheran Church–Missouri Synod, C. F. W. Walther, in 1884 and 1885 delivered a series of thirty-nine evening lectures to his students at Concordia Seminary, St. Louis, on this subject. These lectures have been published in English under the title, *The Proper Distinction Between Law and Gospel.* This book has had a great influence on American Lutheranism. Lutheran catechisms often treat the distinction between law and gospel at the very beginning, or close to the beginning, of the instruction course. Before the confirmand begins the study of doctrine in detail, he first of all becomes acquainted with the doctrine of Scripture and its verbal and plenary inspiration. The second great principle he learns is that law and gospel are "the two great doctrines of the Bible," and that there is a great difference between them.

The doctrine of law and gospel is, to Lutheran theology, one of the greatest and most basic paradoxes of Christianity.

Lutheranism stresses the paradoxical nature of the Christian faith, particularly as it is exemplified by the distinction between law and gospel. Because of this some have tried to draw a parallel between the doctrines of orthodox Lutheranism and Kierkegaardian neo-orthodoxy. The similarity between them is more apparent than real. And it is just here, in the matter of law and gospel, that conservative Lutheranism finds the greatest void in the Danish pessimist. It is strange, in a way, that Kierkegaard, who delighted in paradox, never discovered or understood very clearly the basic paradox of the Christian religion. J. T. Mueller has well said that Kierkegaard

> never came to a clear knowledge of the basic difference between Law and Gospel, but consistently mingled Law and Gospel. Ultimately Kierkegaard's entire teaching was law. Christianity to him was not essentially trust in Christ and the blessed rejoicing which flows from reliance on Christ, but asceticism, self-imposed suffering, work righteousness.[72]

Dr. Walther, at the very beginning of his *Law and Gospel*, told his students

> Comparing Holy Scripture with other writings we observe that no book is apparently so full of contradictions as the Bible, and that not only in minor points, but in the principal matter, in the doctrine how we may come to God and be saved.[73]

He called attention to this fact again and again. At one place he said that "the entire Scriptures seem to be made up of contradictions, worse than the Koran of the Turks."[74]

The *Apology to the Augsburg Confession* says that the law and the gospel must be kept as far apart as the heavens are above the earth.[75] The *Formula of Concord* asserts that if this distinction is not kept clear there can be no true teaching in the church.[76] Because Kierkegaard did not keep the distinction clear, conservative Lutheranism looks upon him as a false prophet and rationalist, although he would undoubtedly be surprised to hear this judgment. J. T. Mueller says of him,

> His theology is not rooted in Scripture and the Christian creeds, but in a new norm of Christianity which basically is rationalistic and therefore anti-Christian; . . . he taught a rationalistic enthusiasm which one-sidedly, and even wrongly so, emphasized sin without pointing out to his readers how they might become free from sin.[77]

In order to set forth the distinction between law and gospel in a concrete way, we add one more chart, in which statements of law and gospel are set over against each other to show the contrast between them.

Law	Gospel
1. The law is written in the heart of man, and is therefore known by nature (Romans 2:15).	1. The gospel is a mystery unknown to man by nature (I Corinthians 2:7ff; Romans 16:25).
2. The law demands perfect obedience from men (Genesis 17:1; Matthew 5:48).	2. The gospel makes no demands but only offers the grace of God to men (Ephesians 2:8,9).
3. The law promises salvation and life to those who obey all its demands (Luke 10:28).	3. The gospel promises salvation to those who have broken the law (Acts 16:31).

4. The law says that the
doers of the law shall
be justified
(Romans 2:13).

4. The gospel says that
those who have not
kept the law shall be
justified (Romans 4:5),
and that a man is justi-
fied without the deeds
of the law
(Romans 3:28).

5. The law says that God
will not forgive sin nor
acquit the sinner
(Joshua 24:19;
Nahum 1:3).

5. The gospel says that
God has acquitted all
men, that he has for-
given the sins of the
world (Romans 5:18;
2 Corinthians 5:19).

6. The law says that every
sinner is to be cursed
(Galatians 3:10).

6. The gospel says that
all the families of the
earth are blessed in
Christ (Genesis 22:18;
Galatians 3:16).

7. The law says that
God hates sinners
(Psalm 5:5; 11:5;
Hosea 9:15).

7. The gospel says that
God loves all men
(John 3:16).

8. The law says that God
is angry with sinners
(Nahum 1:2;
Romans 1:18).

8. The gospel says
that God is favorably
disposed toward all
men and reconciled
to all men (Titus 2:11;
2 Corinthians 5:19).

9. The law has the effect
of arousing men
against God
(Romans 4:15).

9. The gospel has the
effect of reconciling
men with God
(2 Corinthians 5:20).

10. The law terrifies men and is intended to terrify them (Exodus 20:18f.).

10. The gospel is intended to cast out all fear. "Fear not!" (Luke 2:10, et al.).

11. The law must be preached to make the comfortable distressed (Romans 3:20).

11. The gospel must be preached to make the distressed comfortable (Isaiah 40:1).

It must be borne in mind that both doctrines are solidly based on the inspired Word of God. Both are in every sense a word of God. Both are therefore true, and we must say that they are eternally true. If either of these doctrines were to become untrue, God would be a liar. Even Jesus said that he had not come to destroy the law. And St. Paul said that we establish the law by the preaching of grace, although it would appear that the law somehow becomes void in the gospel.

If both law and gospel are permitted to stand thus unmodified side by side, it is very clear that we have more than a slight variation of opinion on our hands. Men have struggled in countless ways to resolve the paradox. Some, like the gross religious evolutionists, simply say that in ancient times God was thought of as an avenging Deity, but now we have learned to picture God to ourselves as a kind and gracious Father. In other words, they assign the law to one period of the history of the world and the gospel to another period.

Others seek to solve the problem by saying that the two doctrines belong into different periods of a man's life, that in the pre-conversion state a man needs to hear the law, but that after conversion, only the gospel should be preached. This position is called antinomianism.

Still others attempt a solution by saying that the first set of passages is intended to mirror God's attitude toward the reprobate and the second set of passages is intended for those whom he has chosen for himself. In Calvinism, this tendency surfaces in the interpretation of the gospel passages, so that they are interpreted to mean that "God so loved the world" of the elect, that "he died for all" the elect, and that he tasted "death for every man" that is elect. In Lutheran circles, this tendency sometimes turns up in the interpretation of the law passages, so that "God hates all workers of iniquity," is made to mean that God hates all workers of iniquity who are impenitent. In both cases words are added to the words of Scripture to make them "clear" to reason.

The most common resolution of the difficulty is one which destroys both law and gospel, so that neither any longer says what it originally said. There are those, for example, who say that since Christ came God no longer demands complete obedience from men, but that he is satisfied if we do the best that we can. This is a watering down of the demands of God until they fall midway between his demands in the law, which call for perfection, and his demands in the gospel, which call for nothing. But this is no longer the word of God.

There are others who make the promises of the gospel conditional. They will say that God is now willing to forgive us provided we have the proper attitude, that God will be gracious to us *if* we repent, or *if* we believe, or *if* we are contrite, or *if* we are willing to amend our sinful lives. Bainton says, "That *if* bothered Luther," [78] and it bothers an orthodox Lutheran to this day because it is so easily understood as indicating a cause on account of which God forgives us or a condition that man must fulfill before he can be forgiven. There are "ifs" in the law, but not in the gospel. This sort of methodology in preaching and teaching is called, in Lutheran theology, a mixing of law and gospel.

But Lutheranism will have none of this. A true Lutheran will find it difficult to imagine a Christmas sermon, or an Easter sermon, in which no mention is made of sin and of death and of hell. Christmas and Easter are great occasions for preaching the gospel, but the gospel means little without the law. Unless men know that they are sick, they will not know that they need a doctor.

Both law and gospel must be allowed to stand without modification, in spite of all their apparent contradictions. Yet, Dr. Walther is perfectly correct when he says in his *Law and Gospel*, "There are no contradictions in Scripture."[79] What looks like a contradiction to reason the believer accepts in childlike faith as perfectly harmonious divine truth.

Take a few of the seemingly contradictory statements of law and gospel to the foot of the cross in faith, and there see how perfectly they are joined. God threatens to punish every sinner. This he did through the vicarious atonement which his Son made on the cross. When Christ died as a sinner, he bore our sins. We died with him. Therefore God now forgives us in him. The law also demands perfect obedience from man. But this perfect obedience has been rendered vicariously through him who said that he had come to fulfill the law, to fulfill all righteousness. Christ's obedience is the obedience of all men, as Adam's sin is the sin of all men. Thus he met the demands of the law, and we are justified as doers of the law through what he has done. Likewise, God threatens to curse the sinners, but Jesus was made a curse for us. Therefore we are blessed in him.

Without the doctrine of vicarious atonement there can be no reconciliation of law and gospel, and without faith in the vicarious atonement men will never arrive at a solution to the paradox of law and gospel. This, however, is not a rational solution devised to satisfy reason. The vicarious atonement itself is an offense to reason. To the natural reason of man, which even the believer will carry with him to the grave, the biblical message is foolishness (1 Corinthians 2:14). In God's great revelation of his name to Moses at Mount Sinai he revealed himself as the God who forgives all sin and the God who punishes all sin (Exodus 34:6,7). He is both a God of infinite justice and revenge and a God of infinite love and mercy. To human reason this will always be an insoluble conundrum—one that can only be solved by making either God's love and grace or his justice and righteousness less than infinite.

But for the Christian believer God has at the cross of Christ found a way to demonstrate both his perfect avenging justice and his perfect forgiving grace. The "foolishness of God" thus shows itself to be "wiser than men" (1 Corinthians 1:21-25). And once a man has accepted that "foolishness" as divine wisdom because a new way of thinking has been created in him by the creative working of the Holy Ghost, that which looked like gross nonsense now appears to be the greatest wisdom, and what appeared to be an impossible contradiction is accepted as divine truth.

There is yet another perspective from which to view this matter. Man was created for heaven, and by his sin he damned himself to hell. Now he needs the law to show him his wretched state, and he needs the gospel to show him the way out of his impossible situation. He needs the law to destroy his pride in his own character, achievements, and works. He needs the gospel to overcome the despair which follows when he finds that he stands naked and alone before God. He needs the law to destroy his faith in himself. He needs the gospel to build his faith in God. What appears impossible to fit together on paper fits perfectly in the human heart.

We see, then, how this paradox is resolved in utmost simplicity for the believer. And we have the certain hope that the light of glory will finally illuminate and resolve many of the other paradoxes of the Christian faith. Whatever still remains a mystery, we shall happily contemplate with the holy angels (1 Peter 1:12).

I know my faith is founded
On Jesus Christ, my God and Lord;
And this my faith confessing,
Unmoved I stand upon his Word.
Man's reason cannot fathom
The truth of God profound;
Who trusts her subtle wisdom
Relies on shifting ground.
God's word is all-sufficient,
It makes divinely sure;
And trusting in its wisdom,
My faith shall rest secure.[80]

CHAPTER VII

SUMMARY

Luther's theological position is often called irrational. His writings contain strong language in condemnation of reason, but he also had many things to say in praise of the rational faculty which God has implanted in man. To understand his position in this matter, we must view it in the light of his scholastic background. From William of Occam he had learned, through his teachers at Erfurt, to look upon reason as totally incompetent in matters of religion. This position was the very opposite of that held by Thomas and the great majority of the later scholastics, who had exalted reason and had given it a position of prominence in theology. Luther held Thomistic and Aristotelian philosophy to be the chief source of woe for the church catholic.

Luther did not entirely deny reason the capacity of knowing God. But he did hold that God was not directly in contact with reason. God is hidden. Man can not and could not, since the Fall, bear the sight of the majestic God. Therefore to reveal himself to man, God puts on a disguise, a mask, behind which he hides his glory. These masks are the works of God in nature, and the word and sacraments.

Man still is unable to read the revelation of God correctly because of his depraved and fallen condition. This does not mean, however, that the so-called "proofs" for the existence of God are invalid or useless. Every man is born with an innate knowledge of God and of God's will. This knowledge man can ignore or eradicate only with difficulty. That men know there is a God is simply an historical fact. The cosmological, teleological, historical, ontological and moral "proofs" serve mightily to stimulate this knowledge into consciousness.

Still Luther lays little weight on this natural knowledge, because the approach of reason to the knowledge of God can never progress beyond the assurance of a high degree of probability. This does not truly meet man's need, because man needs sure knowledge. The existence of evil militates against the conviction which is wrought by the "proofs." Finally, every conclusion based on rational argument can be overthrown again by rational argument.

Even if this knowledge were sure, it would not be sufficient. It is not enough to know that there is a God. I must know that he is my God, my Lord, and my Savior. Men can know that there is a God; but only by revelation, and not by reason, can they know that he is well-disposed toward them.

Moreover, the natural knowledge of God is always legalistic. Man, by nature, believes that God is a God who punishes the wicked and rewards the righteous. Such knowledge can result only in presumptuous pride or in despair. Men know what is right, but they do not have the power to do it.

Natural knowledge helps to maintain decency and order in the world. While it is not a step toward the true knowledge, as Thomism holds, yet it does provide a point of contact with the unbeliever.

As man does not know God, so also he, as long as he remains an unbeliever, does not know God's creation. The origin and destiny of men and of the world can never be known except by revelation and faith. The same is true of efficient and final causes. Men, by reason, can know only material and formal causes. And the only source of adequate and true knowledge of God and of nature is to be found in the revelation of God in Holy Scripture.

Reason can never be the source of true knowledge of God and of the world. Still, when it is used properly it is an excellent instrument. Luther called reason a great gift of God and said that its value cannot be estimated.

The Fall did not destroy reason as such. Reason is not a part of the image of God, which was lost in the Fall. The heathen, who are without the Holy Spirit, make excellent use of reason. The sphere of reason is this present world. Luther admired the accomplishments of the heathen in the area of economics and government.

Even in theology reason has a place. It is to be the instrument for apprehending the meaning of God's revelation. Therefore Luther wanted Aristotle's *Logic* to remain one of the textbooks in the revised curriculum of the German universities.

The revelation of God comes through human speech. The languages are therefore to be studied diligently. Luther turned from the allegorical method of interpreting Scripture to a strictly grammatical approach to Biblical exegesis. He maintained that the Scriptures are to be interpreted in a natural way—that is, the words are to be permitted to say exactly what they intend to say. The context must be given proper weight. To discover the meaning it is not necessary to be specially enlightened by the Holy Ghost.

For the work of studying the Bible, it is necessary to employ reason. Thus reason becomes an excellent tool, or servant, for theology. Luther uses syllogistic reasoning repeatedly in drawing doctrinal conclusions. But reason must always remain subject to the Word. Reason which follows the Word becomes reason illumined by Scripture and informed by faith.

Man remains a rational creature also after conversion. Faith is an intellectual process—that is, it involves the use of the rational faculties with which man was created.

When Luther attacked reason, he had in mind especially the tendency of reason to set itself up as a judge over the truth of God's Word. While he approves the ministerial use of reason, he totally outlaws its magisterial use.

Reason judges on the basis of the evidence furnished by the senses. It is always inclined to judge by what it sees and feels. But faith has to do with things which are not seen. Therefore reason is completely incompetent to judge in theology. Besides this, the experience of any given man is so limited that it can at best form an inadequate basis for judging. Reason always makes the mistake of constructing universals out of particulars, and then it uses its fabricated universals as a basis on which it judges the truth of God's Word. This, says Luther, is absurd.

It is true that to human reason the revelation of God often appears to be foolish and impossible. The real presence of the body and blood of Christ in the Lord's Supper, the person of Christ, the resurrection of the body—are all absurdities to human reason, which judges by what it sees. Here faith must simply put reason to death and refuse to listen to it for even one moment.

Luther believed that natural reason also includes an innate conception of a legalistic way of salvation. All men by nature believe that they are saved by obeying the law. Thus this *opinio legis* always stands in the way of the acceptance of the gospel. Here reason must be sacrificed daily, even by the believer.

Luther holds that there are many truths of Scripture which cannot be reconciled with man's reason. The incarnation, he says, is philosophically impossible, for in it we have the joining of the finite and the infinite in one and the same person. Luther resists every attempt to separate the two natures in Christ in any way. In line with this, he strongly insists on the real presence of the body and blood of Christ in the Lord's Supper.

Luther saw a similar paradox in conversion. He believed in the total depravity of man and in the complete bondage of the will in spiritual things. He also held firmly to the universal will of grace, whereby God wants all men to be saved. He recognized that here the mind of man is faced with an insoluble mystery.

The great paradox in Scripture is the apparent contradiction between law and gospel. These two doctrines, which are both truly the Word of God and eternally true, are completely different from one another. They are more different from each other than contradictories, but they are perfectly joined together in the human heart, which needs them both. The law keeps man from pride, the gospel guards him against despair. Moreover, they are reconciled through the Mediator, Christ. Reason must simply learn in these matters to remain subject to the Word.

From what has been said, it is possible to anticipate the direction that Luther's thought will take in the matter of defending the Christian faith. Man must not seek out the truths of God by speculation. Neither is it in the province of reason to explain the truth of God or to justify his ways. This in itself is already a blasphemous presumption. We are not to ask why God acts thus and so. Nor are we bound to explain the whys of the Christian faith to those who demand this of us. Because the Christian faith in so many areas presents us with paradox and because the truth of God is beyond the confines of experience (faith has to do with things not seen), therefore the way of analogy, as an effort to explain or to justify the ways of God to men, is closed for Luther. He does not reject every analogy. Some analogies may be very useful, but they prove nothing. The best we can hope for from them is that they will serve as illustrations. Many analogies may be downright misleading.

Men are not brought to accept the truth of the Christian faith by rational argument. This is clearly illustrated by the Bible's doctrine of infant baptism, which is the means by which children are brought to faith.

To make the gospel reasonable to unconverted man in an effort to bring about his acceptance of that gospel is therefore the height of folly. Such efforts can only result in a change in the gospel, consequently a destruction of the gospel. It is man's reason that needs to be changed. Precisely because the gospel is a message which is not in conformity with reason, faith is required, for faith believes what reason cannot see. When unbelievers said to Luther that the Christian doctrine made no sense, Luther agreed that it made no sense to unconverted, unenlightened human reason.

The best defense of Scripture is Scripture itself. When men ask for proof of the truth of Christian doctrines, we are simply to quote the Bible passages which teach these doctrines. If men do not accept the doctrines of the Christian faith on the authority of the Bible, we are not even to desire their assent on other grounds. The Christian faith is not to be defended by rational argumentation.

But again, this does not mean that we are not to employ reason in the struggle with the enemies of the faith. Every argument of reason can be overthrown with an argument from reason. We may use reason to show the unbeliever the untenableness of his position and the unwarranted nature of his conclusions. In this area we often hear Luther call his adversaries unreasonable.

Luther's antirationalistic position has maintained itself in the Lutheran Church only with the greatest difficulty. Melanchthon led the Lutheran Church away from Luther's position into rationalism. Most Lutherans today should really be called Melanchthonians.

Lutheranism has always valued reason highly as an instrument of knowledge. Faith is neither anti-intellectual nor extra-intellectual. The rational processes and faculties of man are involved in the communication and apprehension of divine truth. God works in man as in a rational creature, and not in the same way that he works in a stone or a block of wood.

Still Lutheranism, where it is true to the position of the great reformer, refuses to permit reason to sit in judgment on the truth of God's Word. Nor does it allow reason to supply the standards and the principles by which the Scriptures are to be interpreted. The antirationalism of Lutheran theology is especially evident in its doctrines of the real presence, of the person of Christ, of conversion and election, and of preservation in the faith.

The greatest paradox, however, is the apparent contradiction between law and gospel. The proper distinction between law and gospel has always been one of the chief aims of Lutheran theology. The one tells us that God hates men and the other that God loves these same men. The one says that God will damn every sinner and the other that God has forgiven every sinner. But the difficulty is resolved in the cross of Christ and the vicarious atonement, which is known only by faith, and in which both law and gospel find perfect fulfillment.

True Lutheranism insists that men must take their reason captive and follow wherever the Word of God leads, even though what it says may appear to be impossible and absurd to reason. In fact, wherever preachers preach a gospel which is no longer a stumblingblock to the Jews and foolishness to the Greeks, we can be sure that they no longer have the gospel of Jesus Christ. The things of the Spirit of God are foolishness to the natural man.

Epilogue

When God led Israel out of Egypt, he led them in a way that seemed most foolish to human reason. The land of Palestine lay to the north, and he led them to the south. The easy road lay along the coast of the Mediterranean Sea, and he led them through the desert. And finally Moses and the children of Israel, by following the cloud that God gave to guide them, came to the place where they found themselves in an absolutely impossible predicament. Before them lay the Red Sea, to their left the trackless, waterless desert, to the right only more dry sand, and behind them the thunder of Pharaoh's horses and chariots.

And Israel murmured.

So the fiery, cloudy pillar which God has given to men to lead them on their journey through this world often leads us into intellectual difficulties. To follow God's Word is to become a fool in the eyes of men—to do and to think and to say what no man in his "right mind" would say and think and do. The "foolishness of preaching" is still as much foolishness to modern man as it was two thousand years ago. And men reject the gospel not because they are wiser than their fathers, but because they are still as wicked as their fathers were.

Often it appears to the Christian theologian that his adversaries have him in a corner from which there is no escape. He cannot give an answer that will satisfy reason unless he takes the logical route, the easy road from Egypt to Palestine. But once he takes that road he will fall an easy prey to the enemy.

If Israel had chosen the route that men would have chosen, Pharaoh's army would have had an easy road on which to pursue them. There would have been no Red Sea for them to cross. But once they did cross the Sea, it closed over the heads of Pharaoh's soldiers. Then the impassable barrier stood no more before Israel, closing off their escape from Egypt, but behind them, shutting off pursuit from Egypt.

So Israel was saved.

And when the light of the Word leads us into a place where we see only the Red Sea before us, the desert to the right of us, the desert to the left of us, and the armies of Pharaoh behind us, we must learn to stand still and wait to see the glory of the Lord. He led us into this difficulty with his Word. Therefore it is his work, and not ours, to lead us out. And he will. He is our God, and his Word is still the only guide to the Promised Land.

SOLI DEO GLORIA

Bibliography

Bainton, Roland, *Here I Stand* (1950).

Bente F., *"Warum sollen wir uns auch in der Zukunft dem modernen Fortschritt in der Kirche ernstlich widersetzen?"* in *Synodal-Bericht des Westlichen Districts* (Concordia, 1897).

_____ . "Historical Introductions to the Symbolical Books," *Concordia Triglotta* (1921).

Beto, G., "The Marburg Colloquy of 1529: A Textual Study," *Concordia Theological Monthly* (Feb 1945).

Boehmer, H., *Luther in the Light of Recent Research* (1916).

Brunner, Emil, *Revelation and Reason* (1946).

Calvin, J., *Institutes*

Carnell, E. J., *An Introduction to Christian Apologetics* (1956).

Casserley, J. V. Langmead, *The Christian in Philosophy* (1951).

De Wolf, L. Harold, *The Religious Revolt Against Reason* (1949).

Edwards J., "The Freedom of the Will," in Mueider and Sears, *The Development of American Philosophy* (1940).

Engelder, Arndt, Graebner, Mayer, *Popular Symbolics* (1934).

Engelder, Th., *Reason or Revelation?* (1941).

_____ . "The Reformed Doctrine of the Lord's Supper," *Concordia Theological Monthly*, X, 9 (Sept 1939).

Graebner, Theodore, *Predestination and Human Responsibility* (no notice of publisher or date).

Haentzschel, A., *The Great Quest* (1953).

Hagenbach, K., *Dogmengeschichte* (1867).

Hodge, C., *Systematic Theology* (1876).

Hoyer, Th., "The Grace of God," in Th. Laetsch, *The Abiding Word*, II (1947).

Hutchison, J., *Faith, Reason, and Existence* (1956).

Kirchengesangbuch fuer Evangelisch-Lutherische Gemeinden (Concordia).

Kierkegaard, S., *On Authority and Revelation* (1955).

McGiffert, A. C., *History of Christian Thought* (1953).

McKeon, R., *Selections from Medieval Philosophers*, II (1930).

Meusel, C., *Kirchliches Handlexikon* IV (1894).

Mueller, J. T., *Christian Dogmatics* (1934).

——————. "Soeren Aaby Kierkegaard," *Concordia Theological Monthly* (Dec 1945).

Petty, Orville A., *The Laymen's Foreign Mission Inquiry, China*, Supplementary Series, V, ii (1933).

Pieper, Franz, *Christian Dogmatics* (1950).

Plass, Ewald, "Synergism," in Th. Laetsch, *The Abiding Word*, II (1947).

Preus, Robert, *The Inspiration of Scripture* (1955).

Ramm, B., *Types of Apologetic Systems* (1953).

Saarnivaara, Uuras, *Luther Discovers the Gospel* (1951).

Schmid, H., The *Doctrinal Theology of the Lutheran Church* (1876).

Schwiebert, E. G., *Luther and His Times* (1950).

Stoeckhardt, G., *Commentary on St. Paul's Letter to the Ephesians* (1952).

Thiel, R., *Luther* (1955).

Van Til, Cornelius, *Christian Apologetics* (1939).

Walther, C. F. W., *Law and Gospel* (1929).

Watson, Philip, *Let God Be God!* (1949).

Wente, W., "Conversion," in Th. Laetsch, *The Abiding Word*, I (1946).

Wieman and Meland, *American Philosophies of Religion* (1936).

References

KEY TO ABBREVIATIONS

Apol. — *Apology of the Augsburg Confession*

BR — *Briefwechsel* in *WA*

EA — *Erlangen Ausgabe* (Erlangen edition of Luther's works)

ELH — Evangelical Lutheran Hymn-Book

FC — Formula of Concord (Epitome)

SA — *Smalcald Articles*

SD — *Formula of Concord* (Solid Declaration)

SL — St. Louis (Walch II) edition of Luther's works

TLH — *The Lutheran Hymnal*

TR — *Tischreden* in *WA*

WA — *Weimar Ausgabe* (Weimar edition of Luther's works)

Chapter I

Page   Note

I - I   *WA* 10,I,I,271; 51,123

I - 2   *WA* 51,130; 16,42f; 40,I,204

I - 3   *WA* 40,I,362

I - 4   *WA* 40,3,612

I - 5   *WA* 39,I,176; 47,813

I - 6   *WA* 39,2,24; 39,I,175

I - 7   Bainton, 125

2 - 8   *Time*, 20 Aug 1956, p 48

2 - 9   *WA* 42,107

2 - 10 *WA* 40,2,371

2 - 11 *WA* 42,138

2 - 12 *TR* 5,25

3 - 13 *WA* 39,2,6

3 - 14 *WA* 6,176

3 - 15 *WA* 6,186

3 - 16 *WA* 6,187

3 - 17 *WA* 10,I,I,609

4 - 18 *WA* 10,I,I,584

4 - 19 *WA* 10,I,2,73f

4 - 20 *WA* 6,457; 7,739

4 - 21 *WA* 1,509

4 - 22	*WA* 1,221
4 - 23	*Ibid.*
4 - 24	*WA* 10,1,1,584
4 - 25	*WA* 1,226
5 - 26	*WA* 7,739
5 - 27	*WA* 30,3,500
5 - 28	*Ibid.*
5 - 29	*TR* 1,118
5 - 30	*WA* 7,739
5 - 31	*WA* 8,127
6 - 32	*Ibid.*
6 - 33	*TR* 2,193
6 - 34	Schwiebert, 54; see Boehmer, 180
6 - 35	Saarnivaara, 54
6 - 36	*WA* 6,183
6 - 37	SL 15,413
6 - 38	Hagenbach, 466
6 - 39	McKeon, 412ff
6 - 40	McGiffert, 306-308
6 - 41	*WA* 1,509
7 - 42	*WA* 10,1,2,74
7 - 43	*WA* 42,5
7 - 44	*WA* 1,28
7 - 45	*WA* 44,704
7 - 46	*WA* 10,1,1,567
10 - 47	cp *Apol.* IV, 48-60

11 - 48	Brunner, 421
11 - 49	*FC* XI, 28ff
12 - 50	*SA* III, viii, 10
12 - 51	*WA* 40,2,26

Chapter II

Page   Note

13 - 1	Watson, 76
13 - 2	Schwiebert, 692f
13 - 3	*WA* 42,9
13 - 4	*WA* 1,576
13 - 5	*WA* 20,520
14 - 6	*WA* 18,684
14 - 7	*WA* 18,685
15 - 8	*WA* 18,690
15 - 9	*WA* 42,625; cp. 25,393
15 - 10	*WA* 40,1,77
15 - 11	Watson, 95
15 - 12	*WA* 42,652
15 - 13	*WA* 43,239
15 - 14	*TR* 1,72
15 - 15	*WA* 47,545
15 - 16	*WA* 47,543f
16 - 17	*TR* 2,106
16 - 18	*WA* 1,138
17 - 19	*WA* 42,294
17 - 20	*WA* 38,524

17 - 21	WA 42,9
18 - 22	WA 42,9f
18 - 23	WA 42,294; 43,231
18 - 24	WA 43,231
18 - 25	WA 42,624
18 - 26	WA 42,11
19 - 27	WA 43,240
19 - 28	WA 42,294f
19 - 29	WA 42,11
19 - 30	WA 43,231
19 - 31	TR 2,366
20 - 32	WA 16,144
20 - 33	WA 47,540
20 - 34	WA 22,376; 51,150; 39,2,340
20 - 35	WA 14,113
20 - 36	WA 42,9f
20 - 37	WA 43,276
21 - 38	WA 42,93
21 - 39	WA 39,1,175ff
21 - 40	WA 42,45
21 - 41	WA 42,46
21 - 42	WA 10,1,1,528
22 - 43	WA 42,46f
22 - 44	WA 10,1,1,202
23 - 45	WA 40,1,294
23 - 46	WA 42,510

23 - 47	WA 42,96
23 - 48	WA 16,143
23 - 49	WA 16,147
23 - 50	WA 43,241
24 - 51	WA 42,107f
24 - 52	WA 10,1,2,298
25 - 53	Thiel, 390
25 - 54	WA 40,1,410
25 - 55	Watson, 76f
26 - 56	Hutchison, 150
27 - 57	WA 1,355
28 - 58	WA 42,4
28 - 59	WA 16,447
29 - 60	WA 19,205f
29 - 61	WA 19,207
29 - 62	WA 46,666
29 - 63	WA 46,670
30 - 64	WA 39,1,175ff; cp 21,509
30 - 65	WA 46,670
30 - 66	WA 46,666
30 - 67	WA 40,1,607
31 - 68	WA 19,205
31 - 69	WA 24,640
32 - 70	Casserley, 84
32 - 71	Watson, 84
32 - 72	WA 21,509
32 - 73	WA 21,510

32 - 74	*WA* 21,510f	40 - 102	*Ibid.*
33 - 75	*WA* 51,150	41 - 103	*WA* 42,509
33 - 76	*WA* 51,156	41 - 104	*Ibid.*
33 - 77	*WA* 39,2,340	41 - 105	*WA* 42,409
33 - 78	*WA* 46,666	42 - 106	*WA* 19,206
33 - 79	*WA* 40,3,322	42 - 107	*WA* 21,509; cp. p. 12
33 - 80	*WA* 21,509		
34 - 81	*WA* 42,408-409	42 - 108	*WA* 43,240
34 - 82	*WA* 42,292	43 - 109	*WA* 46,667
35 - 83	*WA* 46,666	43 - 110	*WA* 46,667-669
35 - 84	*WA* 19,206	43 - 111	*WA* 46,669-670
35 - 85	*WA* 46,667-668	44 - 112	*WA* 40,1,607
35 - 86	*WA* 46,668	44 - 113	*WA* 22,376
36 - 87	*WA* 39,2,320ff	45 - 114	*Ibid.*
37 - 88	*WA* 43,240	45 - 115	*WA* 39,1,180
37 - 89	*WA* 40,3,71	45 - 116	*WA* 14,588
38 - 90	*TR* 1,530	45 - 117	*WA* 51,151
38 - 91	Carnell, 113	46 - 118	*WA* 21,510
38 - 92	De Wolf, 119	46 - 119	*WA* 42,292
38 - 93	*SL* 9,507	46 - 120	*WA* 31,2,268
38 - 94	*WA* 10,3,357	46 - 121	*WA* 42,292
38 - 95	*WA* 28,91	47 - 122	*WA* 51,150
38 - 96	Brunner, 340	47 - 123	*WA* 44,591
39 - 97	*Ibid.*, 8	47 - 124	*WA* 44,592
39 - 98	*Ibid.*	48 - 125	*Ibid.*
39 - 99	Brunner, 350	48 - 126	*WA* 14,16
40 - 100	*WA* 40,3,321	48 - 127	*WA* 14,16
40 - 101	*Ibid.*	49 - 128	Ramm, 70

49 - 129 BR 2,400-401

50 - 130 WA 10,1,1,528-529

51 - 131 WA 42,486

51 - 132 Ibid.

51 - 133 WA 10,1,1,610

51 - 134 WA 10,1,1,240

52 - 135 WA 40,1,608;
          cp. also 24,640

52 - 136 WA 19,207

53 - 137 see Saarnivaara

53 - 138 WA 43,386

54 - 139 WA 16,354-355

54 - 140 WA 42,291

54 - 141 WA 42,373

54 - 142 WA 42,374

54 - 143 WA 42,291

54 - 144 WA 39,1,180

54 - 145 WA 43,386

55 - 146 WA 40,2,377

55 - 147 Carnell, dust jacket

55 - 148 Carnell, 303

55 - 149 WA 21,514

55 - 150 WA 40,1,603

55 - 151 WA 40,1,42

55 - 152 WA 40,2,7

55 - 153 WA 40,2,377

56 - 154 Watson, 147

56 - 155 WA 42,373

57 - 156 WA 46,670

57 - 157 WA 40,1,138

57 - 158 WA 14,588

57 - 159 WA 10,3,109

57 - 160 WA 22,376

57 - 161 WA 46,670

57 - 162 WA 22,377

58 - 163 WA 10,3,109

58 - 164 WA 40,2,264

58 - 165 Ibid.

59 - 166 Ibid.

59 - 167 WA 16,447

60 - 168 WA 42,511

60 - 169 TR 2,365

60 - 170 WA 42,24

60 - 171 WA 10,1,1,565

61 - 172 WA 10,1,1,567f

61 - 173 WA 42,3f

61 - 174 WA 42,93

62 - 175 WA 39,1,175ff

62 - 176 WA 42,93

62 - 177 WA 42,408

62 - 178 Ibid.

62 - 179 WA 42,409

62 - 180 WA 42,63

62 - 181 WA 42,91

62 - 182 Ibid.

62 - 183 WA 42,92

63 - 184   *WA* 16,113-114

63 - 185   *WA* 40,2,377

64 - 186   *WA* 43,276

64 - 187   Hutchison, 138f

66 - 188   *WA* 42,92

66 - 189   *WA* 40,3,203

66 - 190   *Ibid.*

66 - 191   *Ibid.*

67 - 192   *WA* 42,93-98; 350ff

67 - 193   *WA* 42,94

Chapter III

Page   Note

69 - 1   Watson, 86

70 - 2   *WA* 40,3,612

70 - 3   *WA* 40,3,611

70 - 4   *WA* 47,813

71 - 5   *Ibid.*

71 - 6   *WA* 39,1,176

71 - 7   *WA* 42,408

71 - 8   *WA* 39,1,175

71 - 9   *WA* 10,1,1,528

71 - 10   *WA* 16,354

72 - 11   *WA* 22,108

72 - 12   *WA* 16,261

72 - 13   *WA* 22,42

72 - 14   *WA* 46,56

72 - 15   *WA* 25,393

72 - 16   *WA* 16,353

72 - 17   *WA* 16,354

73 - 18   *WA* 33,127

74 - 19   *WA* 16,260

74 - 20   *Ibid.*

74 - 21   *WA* 43,107

74 - 22   *WA* 44,77

74 - 23   *WA* 42,469

74 - 24   *WA* 44,88

74 - 25   *WA* 24,180

75 - 26   Casserley, 150,170-172

75 - 27   Petty, 280

76 - 28   *WA* 6,457

76 - 29   *WA* 6,458

76 - 30   *Ibid.*

76 - 31   *WA* 15,37f

77 - 32   *WA* 15,38

77 - 33   Haentzschel, 49-50,59

78 - 34   *WA* 16,447

79 - 35   *WA* 15,38f

79 - 36   *WA* 15,38

79 - 37   *TR* 1,191

79 - 38   *WA* 18,180

79 - 39   *WA* 42,138

80 - 40   *WA* 18,180

80 - 41	*WA* 42,3ff	
80 - 42	*WA* 42,97	
80 - 43	*Ibid.*	
80 - 44	*WA* 42,139	
81 - 45	*WA* 18,700	
81 - 46	*TR* 1,587	
81 - 47	*WA* 18,677	
81 - 48	*WA* 40,2,36f	
82 - 49	*WA* 39,2,24	
83 - 50	*WA* 10,1,1,51	
83 - 51	*WA* 47,540	
83 - 52	*WA* 37,44	
83 - 53	*WA* 28,92f	
84 - 54	*WA* 46,683	
84 - 55	*WA* 49,412	
84 - 56	*WA* 49,400	
84 - 57	*WA* 40,2,46	
85 - 58	*WA* 39,2,26	
85 - 59	*TR* 5,616	
86 - 60	*WA* 1,226	
86 - 61	*WA* 39,2,4	
86 - 62	*WA* 39,2,5	
86 - 63	*WA* 39,2,11	
87 - 64	*WA* 39,2,5	
87 - 65	*WA* 40,1,376	
87 - 66	*WA* 40,1,412	
87 - 67	*Ibid.*	
88 - 68	*WA* 40,2,26	

88 - 69	*Ibid.*	
88 - 70	*WA* 40,1,447	
88 - 71	*WA* 6,291	
88 - 72	*WA* 42,452	
89 - 73	*TR* 1,592; 42,608	
89 - 74	*WA* 10,1,1,233	
89 - 75	Edwards, 39	
89 - 76	*WA* 10,1,1,233	
89 - 77	*TR* 2,372	
89 - 78	*WA* 40,1,418	
90 - 79	*TR* 1,191	
90 - 80	*TR* 1,78	
90 - 81	*TR* 6,158	
90 - 82	*TR* 3,102	
91 - 83	*Ibid.*	
91 - 84	*WA* 18,754	
91 - 85	*TR* 3,104	
91 - 86	*WA* 1,355	

Chapter IV

Page	Note	
94 - 1	Bainton, 223	
96 - 2	*WA* 45,511	
96 - 3	*WA* 42,452	
96 - 4	*WA* 36,493	
96 - 5	*WA* 12,637	
96 - 6	*WA* 42,453	
97 - 7	*WA* 36,493	

97 - 8	*WA* 40,3,71	103 - 36	*WA* 18,673
97 - 9	*WA* 10,1,1,613	103 - 37	*WA* 42,118
97 - 10	*WA* 24,173	103 - 38	*WA* 37,44
97 - 11	*WA* 24,174	104 - 39	*WA* 40,1,361
97 - 12	*Ibid.*	104 - 40	*WA* 46,55
97 - 13	*WA* 12,609f	104 - 41	*WA* 42,482
97 - 14	*WA* 12,625	105 - 42	*WA* 51,285
98 - 15	*WA* 17,2,273	105 - 43	*WA* 18,707
98 - 16	*WA* 17,2,202	105 - 44	*WA* 18,707f
98 - 17	*WA* 52,542	105 - 45	*WA* 39,2,254
98 - 18	*WA* 40,3,162	105 - 46	*WA* 39,2,340
98 - 19	*Ibid.*	106 - 47	*WA* 37,43f
98 - 20	*WA* 18,708	106 - 48	*WA* 37,44f
98 - 21	*WA* 10,1,1,611	106 - 49	*TR* 3,62
99 - 22	*WA* 40,1,445	107 - 50	*WA* 36,493f
99 - 23	*WA* 37,43	107 - 51	*WA* 42,118
99 - 24	*TR* 1,183	107 - 52	*WA* 33,264
100 - 25	*WA* 43,395	107 - 53	*WA* 33,267f
100 - 26	*WA* 46,54	108 - 54	*WA* 23,117
100 - 27	*WA* 36,298	108 - 55	*WA* 33,265
100 - 28	*WA* 36,496	108 - 56	*WA* 23,119f
100 - 29	*WA* 36,495	109 - 57	*WA* 23,117
100 - 30	*Ibid.*	109 - 58	*WA* 20,521f
100 - 31	*WA* 36,494	109 - 59	*WA* 18,707
101 - 32	*WA* 40,2,33	109 - 60	*WA* 33,122f
101 - 33	*WA* 37,297	109 - 61	Schwiebert, 704
102 - 34	*TR* 1,592	109 - 62	*WA* 33,123
103 - 35	*Ibid.*	110 - 63	*WA* 39,2,345

110 - 64   WA 39,2,3

110 - 65   WA 47,329

110 - 66   WA 54,64f

110 - 67   WA 36,493

111 - 68   WA 40,1,361

111 - 69   WA 40,1,362

111 - 70   WA 10,1,1,536

111 - 71   WA 40,1,361

112 - 72   Ibid.

112 - 73   WA 40,1,365

112 - 74   TR 2,243

112 - 75   WA 40,1,362

112 - 76   WA 40,1,362f

113 - 77   WA 40,1,370

113 - 78   WA 32,62

113 - 79   WA 32,62f

113 - 80   WA 33,121

114 - 81   WA 51,191

115 - 82   WA 40,1,365

115 - 83   WA 40,1,204

115 - 84   WA 18,729

115 - 85   WA 18,730

115 - 86   WA 25,329;
            40,1,376; 20,613;
            42,452; 40,1,365

115 - 87   WA 40,1,365

115 - 88   WA 40,1,204

116 - 89   Ibid.

116 - 90   WA 40,1,365

116 - 91   TR 1,72

116 - 92   WA 20,613

116 - 93   WA 42,452

117 - 94   WA 40,1,366

117 - 95   WA 40,1,365

117 - 96   WA 40,1,366

117 - 97   WA 40,1,214

117 - 98   WA 40,1,376

117 - 99   WA 40,1,377

118 - 100   WA 17,2,389

118 - 101   WA 24,272

118 - 102   WA 24,449

119 - 103   TR 2,6f

119 - 104   Kierkegaard, 26

120 - 105   WA 40,1,285

120 - 106   WA 18,633

121 - 107   WA 14,247f

121 - 108   WA 10,1,2,303

121 - 109   WA 24,296

121 - 110   WA 24,297

121 - 111   TR 1,585

122 - 112   WA 17,2,13

122 - 113   DeWolf, 141f

123 - 114   Ibid.

123 - 115   Bainton, 223

124 - 116   WA 54,89

124 - 117   WA 47,52

124 - 118   *WA* 40,3,707

124 - 119   *WA* 40,3,705

124 - 120   *WA* 47,52

124 - 121   *WA* 54,91

125 - 122   *WA* 40,3,705

125 - 123   *WA* 40,2,587

125 - 124   *WA* 49,404

125 - 125   *TR* 1,118

125 - 126   *WA* 50,590

125 - 127   *WA* 54,48

126 - 128   *WA* 20,521f

126 - 129   *WA* 39,2,8f

126 - 130   *WA* 39,2,7

127 - 131   *WA* 18,635

127 - 132   *WA* 18,638; 670

127 - 133   *WA* 19,784

127 - 134   *WA* 18,706

127 - 135   *WA* 18,633

127 - 136   *WA* 18,634

127 - 137   *WA* 18,638

128 - 138   *WA* 18,784

128 - 139   *Ibid.*

128 - 140   *WA* 18,770

128 - 141   *WA* 18,706

129 - 142   *WA* 18,784

129 - 143   *WA* 18,633

129 - 144   *WA* 18,786

130 - 145   *WA* 18,769

130 - 146   *WA* 46,678

130 - 147   *WA* 52,637

130 - 148   *TR* 2,584

131 - 149   *TR* 3,94

131 - 150   *WA* 18,686

131 - 151   *WA* 17,1,163

131 - 152   *WA* 52,618

132 - 153   *EA* 54,21ff; cp
            WA 8,69

132 - 154   *WA* 18,786

133 - 155   *WA* 47,540

133 - 156   *WA* 18,706

133 - 157   *WA* 52,637

133 - 158   *WA* 46,682

133 - 159   *WA* 18,686

133 - 160   *WA* 38,557

133 - 161   *WA* 17,1,159

133 - 162   *WA* 17,1,163

133 - 163   *WA* 33,362

133 - 164   *WA* 33,118

133 - 165   *WA* 21; 514;
            33,363

134 - 166   *WA* 33,362

134 - 167   *WA* 42,307

134 - 168   *WA* 40,1,141

134 - 169   *TR* 3,624

135 - 170   *WA* 12,633

135 - 171   *WA* 36,22

135 - 172   WA 40,1,529

135 - 173   WA 40,1,371

135 - 174   WA 18,724f

135 - 175   WA 40,1,371

136 - 176   TR 2,13

136 - 177   WA 40,1,43f

136 - 178   WA 40,1,520

136 - 179   WA 40,1,44

136 - 180   TR, 1,273

136 - 181   WA 18,719

136 - 182   WA 40,2,463

136 - 183   WA 36,22

136 - 184   TR 3,624

137 - 185   WA 40,1,523

137 - 186   WA 40,1,368

137 - 187   WA 40,1,372

138 - 188   Ibid.

138 - 189   WA 39,1,47

138 - 190   WA 40,1,44

139 - 191   WA 40,1,420

Chapter V

Page   Note

141 - 1   WA 6,188

141 - 2   TR 1,69

141 - 3   TR 5,25

142 - 4   Casserley, 148f

142 - 5   WA 33,121f

143 - 6   WA 16,140f

143 - 7   WA 18,709

144 - 8   WA 18,712

144 - 9   see 16,143f;
          47,540

144 - 10 WA 43,77

144 - 11 WA 43,76f

145 - 12 WA 16,141

145 - 13 Watson, 84

146 - 14 WA 43,374

146 - 15 Ibid.

146 - 16 WA 40,1,459

146 - 17 WA 40,1,459f

146 - 18 TR 1,606

147 - 19 WA 40,1,460

147 - 20 WA 47,328

147 - 21 WA 21,512

147 - 22 WA 25,329

147 - 23 WA 28,92

148 - 24 WA 40,2,592

148 - 25 WA 10,1,1,611

148 - 26 Bainton, 65

148 - 27 WA 42,452

149 - 28 WA 10,3,357

149 - 29 Schwiebert, 476

149 - 30 WA 33,284

149 - 31 WA 33,284-287

150 - 32 WA 36,492

150 - 33	WA 18,659
150 - 34	WA 47,330
150 - 35	WA 33,264ff
151 - 36	WA 1,696
151 - 37	TR 1,544
151 - 38	WA 42,453
151 - 39	TR 1,576
151 - 40	WA 17,2,72-82
152 - 41	WA 17,2,84f
152 - 42	WA 17,2,87
152 - 43	TR 3,62
152 - 44	WA 10,1,218
152 - 45	WA 42,486
153 - 46	TR 6,181
153 - 47	Petty, 280
154 - 48	WA 40,3,704
154 - 49	WA 36,492
154 - 50	TR 3,62
154 - 51	WA 40,2,589; 40,2,587
154 - 52	WA 47,328
154 - 53	WA 40,2,374
155 - 54	DeWolf, 36
155 - 55	WA 40,2,593
155 - 56	WA 40,2,589
155 - 57	TR 1,213
155 - 58	WA 10,1,1,152
156 - 59	WA 33,120

156 - 60	WA 40,2,589
156 - 61	WA 18,633
156 - 62	WA 18,784
157 - 63	WA 32,57
157 - 64	WA 37,43
157 - 65	TR 4,578
157 - 66	WA 26,145f
157 - 67	WA 32,58
158 - 68	WA 37,43
158 - 69	WA 41,274
158 - 70	WA 40,2,588
159 - 71	WA 41,274
159 - 72	WA 40,2,589
159 - 73	WA 41,273-274
159 - 74	WA 47,51
159 - 75	WA 41,274
159 - 76	WA 40,2,589
160 - 77	WA 40,2,587
160 - 78	WA 40,2,593
160 - 79	WA 18,186f
160 - 80	TR 1,185
161 - 81	Ibid.
161 - 82	Bainton, 139
161 - 83	Watson, 24
162 - 84	WA 49,412
162 - 85	WA 49,413
162 - 86	WA 41,271
162 - 87	WA 36,204

162 - 88 WA 22,40; see also TR 2,243

162 - 89 WA 10,I,1,613f

162 - 90 Ibid.

163 - 91 WA 42,482

163 - 92 WA 36,526

163 - 93 WA 18,659

163 - 94 WA 36,492

163 - 95 WA 28,91

163 - 96 Ibid.

164 - 97 WA 32,57

164 - 98 WA 32,60

164 - 99 WA 40,2,592

164 - 100 TR 2,243

164 - 101 WA 41,274

165 - 102 WA 47,329

165 - 103 WA 40,2,592

165 - 104 WA 40,2,593

166 - 105 WA 6,291

166 - 106 WA 36,528

166 - 107 WA 23,131

166 - 108 WA 20,770; 22,44

166 - 109 WA 6,291f

167 - 110 WA 12,362

167 - 111 Ibid.

167 - 112 WA 36,526

168 - 113 WA 36,525

168 - 114 Ibid.

168 - 115 WA 36,525-528

169 - 116 TR 1,530

169 - 117 e.g. WA 18,786

169 - 118 WA 18,709

170 - 119 WA 18,709-711

170 - 120 WA 18,672

170 - 121 WA 18,673

171 - 122 Ibid.

171 - 123 WA 18,672f

171 - 124 WA 18,675

172 - 125 WA 47,327

172 - 126 WA 17,2,85

172 - 127 WA 17,2,82-87

172 - 128 TR 3,62

172 - 129 WA 18,187

173 - 130 WA 18,186ff

173 - 131 TR 2,60

174 - 132 WA 6,176

174 - 133 WA 6,184

174 - 134 WA 6,195

174 - 135 WA 6,290

174 - 136 WA 7,712

174 - 137 TR 1,57

175 - 138 WA 54,89

175 - 139 Ibid.

175 - 140 Ibid.

175 - 141 Casserley, 172

176 - 142 WA 40,I,78

176 - 143 *WA* 18,785

177 - 144 *WA* 49,400

177 - 145 *WA* 49,403f

177 - 146 *WA* 49,404

177 - 147 *WA* 49,400

178 - 148 *WA* 49,403f

178 - 149 *TR* 1,381

178 - 150 *WA* 42,452

178 - 151 *WA* 10,1,242

178 - 152 *WA* 52,29

178 - 153 *WA* 40,2,53

179 - 154 *WA* 40,2,54

179 - 155 *WA* 38,510

180 - 156 Hutchison, 93

180 - 157 Ramm, 70

180 - 158 *WA* 10,1,1,611

180 - 159 *WA* 26,164f

181 - 160 DeWolf, 200

181 - 161 Saarnivaara, 124

182 - 162 *TR* 1,25

182 - 163 *WA* 10,1,1,614

182 - 164 *WA* 21,448f

182 - 165 *WA* 40,2,31-33

182 - 166 *WA* 10,3,222

182 - 167 *WA* 33,267

182 - 168 *WA* 10,1,1,611

183 - 169 Walther, 201

183 - 170 *Kirchengesangbuch*, 234:10

183 - 171 *Kirchengesangbuch*, 135:8

183 - 172 quoted by Saarnivaara, 54

Chapter VI

Page   Note

185 - 1   Meusel, 710

185 - 2   Bente, "Historical Introductions," 105

185 - 3   Beto, 82

185 - 4   "Unaltered Augsburg Confession"

186 - 5   "By grace alone," one of the three watchwords of Lutheranism, "by grace alone, by faith alone, by Scripture alone."

186 - 6   *Apol.* IV (II), 9; III,164-168

186 - 7   *Apol.* III, 108

186 - 8   Bente, "Historical Introductions," 93ff

187 - 9   *Ibid.*, 93

187 - 10   *Ibid.*, 105

187 - 11   Preus, 8ff

188 - 12   *SD* II, 62

188 - 13   *Ibid.*, 59

189 - 14 Preus, 9ff; see also Schmid, 45-55

189 - 15 Pieper, 197

189 - 16 J. T. Mueller, *Christian Dogmatics*, 80,92

189 - 17 Bente, *"Warum sollen wir,"* 21

190 - 18 Beto, 76

190 - 19 Walther, 29

190 - 20 quoted by Th. Engelder, "The Reformed Doctrine," 641

191 - 21 Hodge, III, 632

191 - 22 *Ibid.*

191 - 23 Calvin, IV, 17,23

191 - 24 Engelder, Arndt, 95

191 - 25 Engelder, "The Reformed Doctrine," 654

192 - 26 This phrase, which might be translated "the legalistic attitude," is regularly used in Lutheran circles to denote the natural attitude of man which holds that men are saved by keeping the law.

194 - 27 *SD*, VII, 45-47; 92,102,106

194 - 28 *SD*, VII, 106

194 - 29 *SD*, VII, 45

194 - 30 *TLH* 306:5

194 - 31 *TLH* 304:1,5

195 - 32 *TLH* 305:6

195 - 33 see e.g. Wieman, 67

197 - 34 *SD*, VII, 39f

197 - 35 Pieper, II, 120f

198 - 36 *SD*, VII, 45

198 - 37 Engelder, Arndt, 47

198 - 38 *LW* 21,322

198 - 39 *SD*, VII, 24

199 - 40 *ELH* 215:2

199 - 41 *TLH* 167:2

199 - 42 *Kirchengesangbuch*, 88:2

200 - 43 Latin: *intellectum;* German: *Verstand.*

200 - 44 *SD*, VIII, 96

201 - 45 Stoeckhardt, 132

201 - 46 *SD*, II, 3-5

201 - 47 *Ibid.*, II, 8

201 - 48 *SD*, II, 8

202 - 49 Wente, 173

202 - 50 Plass, 304

202 - 51 *SD*, II, 86

202 - 52 *SD*, II, 78

202 - 53   Stoeckhardt, 138:
           the ability not to
           resist

203 - 54   *SD*, II, 49

203 - 55   see e.g. Hoyer,
           224ff and almost
           any other Lutheran
           dogmatics

204 - 56   Hoyer, 229

204 - 57   *Ibid.*

205 - 58   Plass, 305

206 - 59   *SD*, XI, 5

206 - 60   *Ibid.*, 8

206 - 61   *Ibid.*, 28

206 - 62   *Ibid.*, 26

206 - 63   par. 38

206 - 64   *Ibid.*, par. 37; cp
           SD, XI, 41

206 - 65   *SD*, XI, 88

206 - 66   *Apol.* III, 212ff

207 - 67   par. 36

207 - 68   Graebner, 8

208 - 69   *Ibid.*

213 - 70   *TLH* 413

214 - 71   Engelder, *Reason or
           Revelation?* 170

216 - 72   Mueller, "Soeren
           Aaby Kierkegaard,"
           821f

216 - 73   Walther, 6

216 - 74   *Ibid.*, 61

217 - 75   *Apol.* III, (p 173)

217 - 76   *SD*, V, 1f

217 - 77   Mueller, "Soeren
           Aaby Kierkegaard,"
           822

220 - 78   Bainton, 336

221 - 79   Walther, 7

223 - 80   *TLH* 381:1

Index

Scripture Passage Index

CPSIA information can be obtained at www.ICGtesting.com
Printed in the USA
LVOW09s1118031114

411665LV00002B/2/P